Advance praise for *No One's the Bitch*

"The authors have it right—the relationship between mother and step-mother is the one that makes or breaks the wildly extended American families of the 21st century. That's why we have to suck it up and make it work. This book is full of wisdom and practical resources to get you there."

—Marion Winik, author of *Rules for the Unruly:*
Living an Unconventional Life and *The Glen Rock Book of the Dead*

"Brave, bold and right on time, *No One's the Bitch* has the potential to change how step- and blended families get along forevermore. Jennifer and Carol Marine show mothers and stepmothers how to put down the gloves, make peace and become partners. A breakthrough from page one!"

—Izzy Rose, author of *The Package Deal: My (not-so) Glamorous*
Transition from Single Gal to Instant Mom

"Finally! A must-read user's guide for every woman involved in a step-mother/ex-wife relationship. With humor, insight, and unflinching honesty, Jennifer and Carol take you through the process of making one of the trickiest relationships in our culture infinitely easier. Leave the snarking behind! This book will give you the tools to move on and glory in some newfound possibilities."

—Katherine Shirek Doughtie, *The Doughtie Houses Exchange*
(www.thedhx.com) and author of *Aphrodite in Jeans:*
Adventure Tales about Men, Midlife, and Motherhood

"I wish I could have read this book when I was first starting out as a stepmom. If you're stuck in the middle of a mom-stepmom conflict and you're looking for a way to create a peaceful relationship, start with this book. If you're thinking about marrying into a stepfamily or you're in the early honeymoon phase of your stepfamily, this book might shine a light on some of the hidden landmines in stepfamily life and help you successfully navigate through them! This is a groundbreaking book that our families have been waiting for for decades. Where other co-parenting books talk you through how to act differently on the outside, this book holds your hand through opening your heart to a transformation that overflows into your family and your relationship with the other house."

—Jill Doughtie, *The Doughtie Houses Exchange* (www.thedhx.com)

"These straight-shooting, truth-talking, soul-baring women have their priorities right: When mom and stepmom are on the same page everyone wins, most especially the kids! If more parents could do as authors Jennifer and Carol have done, our courts would be far emptier, our kids would be far healthier and all of our futures would be brighter!"

—Benjamin D. Garber, Ph.D., author of
Keeping Kids Out of the Middle

No
One's
the
BITCH

A Ten-Step Plan for the Mother
and Stepmother Relationship

Jennifer Newcomb Marine
and Carol Marine

life

Guilford, Connecticut
An imprint of The Globe Pequot Press

To buy books in quantity for corporate use
or incentives, call **(800) 962–0973**
or e-mail **premiums@GlobePequot.com.**

GPP Life gives women answers they can trust.

GPP Life is an imprint of The Globe Pequot Press.

Text design: Sheryl P. Kober
Layout: Joanna Beyer

Library of Congress Cataloging-in-Publication Data is available on file.

ISBN 978-0-7627-5093-1

Printed in the United States of America

10 9 8 7 6 5 4 3 2 1

For Sophie, Madeleine, and Jacob—we love you.

Contents

Introduction . . . . **xiii**

    Who We Are. . . . . **xiii**

    How We Got Here . . . . **xiv**

    Our Goal. . . . . **xv**

    What to Expect . . . . **xv**

    What You Stand to Gain . . . . **xvi**

Chapter One: Survey the Landscape

(And Get Your Bearings) **1**

    Going about Your Business **1**

    "And To Your Left . . . ". **2**

    A Look Back from Us. **3**

    Common Features of the Stepmom/Ex-Wife Landscape **5**

    Maxine and Stephanie Duke It Out, from Afar **11**

    What about the Man?. **15**

    External Influences **18**

    United by Their Differences **21**

    Extra Reassurance **23**

    Resources to Explore **26**

    As We Leave the Chapter. **27**

Chapter Two: Own Your Own Crap

(What, Me? A Dark Side?). **28**

    Turning the Flashlight On **28**

    A Look Back from Us. **28**

    Disowning Your Relatives **31**

    Top Ten Reasons Not to Even Bother Trying to Get Along

        with the Stepmom or Ex-Wife **34**

    Shadow Self, Up Close **35**

What about the Man?. **43**

Dude, Where's My Trophy? **51**

Emotional Math: Payoffs vs. Costs **51**

Extra Reassurance **55**

Resources to Explore **57**

As We Leave the Chapter. **57**

Chapter Three: Imagine the Benefits

(Dreams Pull You Forward). **58**

Lighter but Stronger! **58**

A Look Back from Us. **58**

A Vital Fuel **61**

What's in It for Me?. **61**

Two Parallel Realities for Maxine and Stephanie **63**

Overview of the Specific Benefits **69**

What about the Man?. **73**

Creating a New Kind of Family Structure **77**

Stepping Back and Assessing **80**

Extra Reassurance **80**

Resources to Explore **82**

As We Leave the Chapter. **82**

Chapter Four: Take Action

(Stretching, Inside and Out) **83**

The Difference between Sitting and Walking **83**

A Look Back from Us. **83**

Things to Ponder Before You Act **85**

What about the Man?. **93**

External Actions **96**

What You're Going to Actually Try **96**

Stuff to Keep in Mind Beforehand **102**

Signaling a Sea Change. **106**

Invite Her for Coffee **107**

Extra Reassurance **111**

Resources to Explore **114**

As We Leave the Chapter. **115**

Chapter Five: Collaborate

(Lighten Your Load—and Hers) **116**

No Singing, Just Drenched. **116**

A Look Back from Us. **116**

A Closer Look at Collaboration **120**

Defensiveness **122**

The Amazing Power of "Just Talking" **125**

What about the Man?. **127**

Consistent Rules between Houses. **129**

Extra Reassurance **134**

Resources to Explore **137**

As We Leave the Chapter. **138**

Chapter Six: Be Accountable

(No One Else to Blame) **139**

Stay in Your Room!. **139**

A Look Back from Us. **139**

A Definition. **144**

The Benefits of Being Accountable **145**

What Accountability Looks Like in Action **148**

Some Additional Challenges to Practicing Accountability. . . **150**

What about the Man?. **151**

Extra Reassurance **152**

Resources to Explore **154**

As We Leave the Chapter. **154**

Chapter Seven: Communicate

(Or, Why Aren't You a Mind Reader?). **155**

    On the One Hand **155**

    A Look Back from Us. **155**

    Communication 101 . . . . **158**

    Consequences of Poor Communication **161**

    What about the Man?. **166**

    Harnessing Good Communication to Increase Two-Family

        Harmony **167**

    Family Meetings **169**

    Extra Reassurance **170**

    Resources to Explore **173**

    As We Leave the Chapter. **173**

Chapter Eight: Regroup

(Dust Off Your Pants When You Fall Down) **174**

    A Pile of Fire Extinguishers **174**

    A Look Back from Us. **174**

    How Many Kinds of Conflict? Let Me Count the Ways . . . **177**

    Help for in the Moment **178**

    Help You Can Use Later **184**

    What about the Man?. **188**

    Other Ideas to Try **189**

    Extra Reassurance **190**

    Resources to Explore **193**

    As We Leave the Chapter. **193**

Chapter Nine: Strengthen

(Bringing out the Best in the Kids) **194**

    A Common Horizon **194**

    A Look Back from Us. **194**

    What Might Stand in the Way **197**

    What about the Man?. **201**

Why Do This? **202**

Examine What They Need **203**

Figure Out How to Make It Happen **204**

One Last Motivator. **206**

Extra Reassurance **206**

Resources to Explore **208**

As We Leave the Chapter. **209**

Chapter Ten: Celebrate and Acknowledge

(Anytime is Springtime). **210**

Shaking Hands over the Fence. **210**

A Look Back from Us. **210**

How Far You've Come **215**

What about the Man?. **216**

Putting Current Problems in Perspective. **217**

Look for More Ways to Bond and Connect **223**

Extra Reassurance **224**

Resources to Explore **225**

As We Leave the Chapter (and the Book) **225**

Index **227**

Acknowledgments **235**

About the Authors **237**

Introduction

It's a nasty word, **BITCH.**

It's one thing if you're standing up in the face of injustice to do the right thing—who cares if anyone thinks you're a bitch? But being thought of as bitch **in general** is another thing altogether.

No one wants that.

And yet, here's the setup between ex-wife and stepmother: The other woman, no matter which side you start from, is **automatically** a bitch. You'll find plenty of ammunition to lob from friends, family, and coworkers—heck, from people you barely even know. Start out any story about "the ex-wife" or "the stepmother" and people have already helped you pull the pin, ready to take her down. The land stretching between mother and stepmother is littered with such landmines. Good luck tiptoeing around them.

And isn't it irritating to know the other side is almost certainly calling you a bitch?!

WHO WE ARE

We've figured out a way to do it otherwise. We don't know everything, but we *do* know a few things. And we'd like to tell you about them, because when we were first starting out, we sure could have used a book like this, and it was nowhere to be found.

We're a mother and stepmother who've cultivated, first, a working relationship, then a friendship, and now a partnership as coauthors. We've been at it for nine years and have seen the two children we both raise stretch out from very small people to now one very tall person and one medium-size, both of whom will probably leave us all in the dust, height-wise. Three years ago, a brand-new baby boy (hi, baby!) was added to our version of an extended family. And so, with wide-eyed wonder, the stepmom became a mom, and the ex-wife became, proudly and gratefully, an honorary aunt.

We've navigated some really tricky territory to get to this point. And we fully realize it's not all pancakes and roses from here on out. When you first meet your ex's beautiful new girlfriend getting off the back of his new motorcycle, her curly hair cutting through the air in slow motion like a model's, you're not exactly set to like her. When the only way she's gotten to know you is through tales of your bad behavior told to her by her perfect romantic partner, well, she's not so sure she's ever going to find one single thing to like about you either.

There are issues of territoriality, competition, jealousy, anger—and grief, loss, and sadness from both ends. Throw money and some legal elements into the mix and you have the perfect combustible material for a really . . . bad . . . family barbecue.

HOW WE GOT HERE

If you were to see our journey thus far from a bird's-eye view, you'd first see two strangers walking separately but concurrently, eyeing each other suspiciously. Then you'd hear some cautious mumbling directed at the other person (*What? I can't hear you! Speak English!*). This would be followed by a few half-hearted attempts at meaningless, polite chit-chat. Still climbing the low hills, you'd see us maybe veering a little closer to each other's path, as we found (surprise!) we actually had some things in common (the children).

Then we'd get distracted by something hard that we had to do together, like deal with a swarm of jungle flies (kids), cross a rushing river (kids), run from wild, howling boars (hungry kids), or construct an intricate, weight-bearing puzzle made solely out of cooked noodles (getting kids to clean up after themselves).

Somewhere along the line, you'd see us letting our guard down ever so s-l-o-w-l-y, and, yes, sometimes it would go right back up, but by the end of the path, we'd have gone through enough stuff together and spent enough time together that we'd be sitting at a coffee shop (in Europe, alone, just us two girls, with lots of money and no men . . . just kidding!) talking over ideas for our book.

Our book, about how we learned to get along.

OUR GOAL

We're not hoping to get every one of you potential Stepmother/ Mother pairs out there to the point of writing a book together (too much competition), but we *are* hoping you can get to a place where you can actually sit down and have coffee with the other woman. Not "the bitch" anymore—just the other woman. (No, not that Other Woman.)

We're hoping we can help you eventually create what we have—a *partnership* where you can discuss issues of parenting—the things that pull and tug at your heart and keep you up at night—with the other person also mothering the children in your life. We're hoping you can bond over shared issues of pride as you watch the little people in your life grow and fall, and get up again, and blossom. That you can both *give and get* sympathy as life gets rough and the parenting inevitably falls by the wayside. But at least you know you won't be judged by the other person, who, luckily, is not waiting around anymore to pounce on your faults like a stealthy mountain lion.

WHAT TO EXPECT

For each chapter of the book, we'll tell you a bit about what it was like for us before, we'll cover some juicy truths that people might be reluctant to talk about, and we'll give you some ideas you can experiment with. We'll talk about the influence of the ex-husband/husband, and we'll mix things up with a variety of fun quizzes and interactive elements to vary the pace. All along the way, you'll have opportunities to journal about your own thoughts and experiences.

We're going to ask you to take a good look around you and get to know where you are, this classically, stereotypically hostile Badlands. We're going to ask you to take a good look at your own crap and own up to all the ways that you've been adding fuel to that big, nasty bonfire. We're going to help you imagine how good it can be and give you something to shoot for.

Whew. Exhausting, huh? You're tired just reading about it, aren't you?

Why slog through so much mud, you ask? Wouldn't it just be easier to grit your teeth and bear the misery? To say, look, face it, no—really, *this* particular other woman really is a total bitch—it's hopeless! You don't know my situation!

The answer to those questions is in school right now, or perhaps sleeping, or maybe playing with blocks or outside on the swing set, or maybe, like most strapping, young American children, is online or watching TV. That's why. The kids. The whole reason you have to deal with the other woman in the first place.

As tired and frayed as this phrase has become, please, *do it for the children.*

Do it so that they don't have to feel stuck in the middle between two warring women (perhaps quietly, but don't kid yourself, you know what children's little radars are like). Do it so that they can have happier birthdays and holidays, more fluency between the stuff that's forever traveling back and forth between their two houses.

Do it so that they can feel like they're not going to be forever damaged for coming from a "broken family"—hey, their family is just wider, spread out over a larger geographical distance. Do it so that your energy and time and wisdom and obsessive compulsions can go where they really should be going—toward giving them the best upbringing you can, with love, consistency, and an eagle eye for the small, but all-so-important details.

Wouldn't you rather pour yourself into that?

WHAT YOU STAND TO GAIN

On a purely selfish level, you'll feel a lot better if you work on cultivating a friendly relationship with the other woman, instead of hating her. Your stomach will feel calmer, your head will feel clearer, and your heart will feel cleaner. And there's something to be said for just generally creating less bile in your life, wouldn't you say?

Your romantic relationship will benefit from the lack of gossip and snide comments and negativity, and that's also good for the kids. You'll be a better mother or stepmother. Your friendships won't sag under the weight of obsessive harping and one-upmanship.

Most important, *you stand to divorce-proof the stepfamily,* and this matters, whether you're the stepmother or the ex-wife. Divorce is an even greater threat for stepfamilies, compared to nuclear families. And it puts the children at risk of going through an additional divorce if traditional acrimony between the two women is not resolved, or at least made manageable.

We'll invite you to think about how you can strengthen and fine-tune your extended family, to create the best possible worlds for your children or stepchildren, to help them develop to their highest potential. We'll set you to brainstorming about how to create a "soft place to fall" for them, a healthy nest from which to grow out into the world.

And all along the way, we hope you'll celebrate and acknowledge your efforts and any progress made, however small, so that you can take little pit stops of rest in the reinvigorating pride of accomplishment.

Not only that, but you're going to be doing something really forward-thinking and important here, you'll be pioneers! Groundbreakers! You're going to be at the forefront of a new, absolutely called-for movement in our culture to create a totally workable extended family. Divorce and remarriage isn't going to go away soon—let's not only make the best of our situations, let's choose to *thrive* in them.

So join us as we walk through this landscape and see how you can improve your own situation, *wherever you may be.* No one has to be the bitch. And it's worth it. You'll see.

A special note

There are some stepmother/mother teams out there who may not *ever* get along. Why are we telling you this *now?* Aren't we trying to convince everyone to be the best of friends? The chummiest of pals? Actually, no. Honestly, some situations are simply beyond the capabilities of any one single person to change or improve.

So how will you know if this situation applies to you?

First, we'll help you see, with razor-sharp accuracy, what you're contributing to the acrimony between you, and we'll give you some techniques for breaking through it. And all along, we'll give you suggestions for what to do if you meet with resistance from the other side. Then, if you work hard to improve the relationship, and after sincere, honest efforts fail, you'll still be in a stronger position after reading this book. You'll be clearer and more grounded in the face of challenges because you'll understand yourself, the other woman, and the entire situation much better. That can only be a good thing and will ultimately help you create peace, security, and stability for yourself and your family.

1

Survey the Landscape

(And Get Your Bearings)

GOING ABOUT YOUR BUSINESS

Imagine you're in your car on your way home. You're taking a path that's perfectly routine and unremarkable. Matter of fact, you're on automatic pilot, not really thinking as you drive, lost in thought.

*Suddenly, you feel a disorienting, **pulling** sensation as the view in front of you seems to fade, then disappear before your eyes. You suddenly find yourself landing hard on the ground of a lovely, green forest. **What in the world** is going on? Are you stuck in a dream? Is this what a psychotic break is like? Was something slipped into your morning coffee?*

The idyllic setting is starkly at odds with how you feel. The sun is slicing through the tall trees, birds are twittering, a squirrel skitters up a trunk in spirals. You hear the sound of moving water.

The air is mild, but you shiver.

Are you on a reality game show? Were you taken from your car and made unconscious and dropped off here, with cameras rolling, waiting for you to wake up? Is anyone going to spring out from behind a tree, yelling, "Gotcha!"?

*You dust the dirt from your hands, stand up, and look around. After a few minutes, you decide to make your way toward the water. You come to the edge of the tree line and blink at the bright sun. The water must be over **there,** where the barest hint of a line bisects the meadow in front of you. Then, farther away, there's another stand of trees.*

You see movement in the forest across the way and the skin on the back of your neck contracts. Someone steps out from the trees and is standing there, staring your way.

What?

No . . . it can't be.

*It's her! **It's the other woman!** It is!*

You dart back into the trees, hoping she hasn't seen you. **Now what are you going to do?**

That's it, you decide. When I find out what channel we're on, **I'm going to kill these people.**

"AND TO YOUR LEFT . . . "

If you're reading this book, then you also know what it's like to unwillingly find yourself in a Strange Land. No one really prepares you for how weird and difficult and unpleasant it is to have an ex-wife or a stepmother stuck in your life. No one seems to understand how disoriented and helpless you sometimes feel, how she seems to insert herself into *everything.* And no one seems to have a clue for how to make it work either, because on the whole, everyone seems pretty miserable.

If you're feeling the need to gather your wits about you, *perfect,* because that's what this chapter's all about. As your tour guides, we'll do that special finger-pointing thing that flight attendants do so well and describe some of the most common problems and feelings that women struggle with in this situation.

We'll tell you a bit about ourselves, essentially stripping down to our skivvies and dancing around the roasted pig at dusk, all in the service of your edification and entertainment. We'll take a look at the ex-husband's role in influencing what happens between the two women. We'll meet an average ex-wife and stepmom, limping along. And we'll examine some external forces that come into play.

Feeling lucky?

By the end of the chapter, you'll have much more of a sense of *normalcy* about all the *lunacy* you may be living with. And even though that's not the same thing as a magic wand that fixes everything, we'll be walking *together* toward a place of calm, on the other side of the chaos.

Yes, you may have found yourself in a crisis, one you never could have anticipated when you scanned the horizon of your romantic future. But within every crisis lies an opportunity to grow and change, sometimes in deep, dramatic, and exciting ways.

JOURNAL

Grab a pencil or pen and answer the following questions to take a closer look at where you are in your mother/stepmother relationship with the other woman.

Do you currently feel like you're in alien territory? _____
_____

Do you ever wish you could press the "reverse" button and escape this situation altogether? _____
_____

Do you wish you had a better sense of the stepmother/ex-wife big picture?_____
_____

A LOOK BACK FROM US

We want you to get to know us too. We lived this stuff—and came out the other side (relatively) unscathed. So in every chapter, we'll jump in briefly and tell you a little story or two.

Jennifer: The very first time I met Carol was in my driveway. It was a beautiful spring day, but despite the searing-blue, cloudless skies and California-like temperature, I believe I had already been sweating bullets for hours in preparation for their visit: *their* being my ex-husband, David, and his new girlfriend. And not just his new girlfriend, but his new girlfriend fourteen years my junior. (Do not spend time looking closely in the mirror before a visit like this. Just sayin'.) I was also internally rolling my eyes at the fact that David had just bought a motorcycle (long since sold). I bolted outside out of super-strung nerves when I heard them pull up.

Ech. There's nothing like pure jealousy to make you feel helplessly sick to your stomach. Carol was pretty, in shape, and I'd already seen her art, so I knew she was talented and creative. She swung a muscular leg over the back of the motorcycle, dismounting like a gymnast, and removed her helmet, shaking out beautiful, light brown curls. I hated her already. I felt something melting in the pit of my stomach, which should have been accompanied by the smell of electrical wires about to catch fire. I wanted to turn around and go home but—oh.

I already was.

There was nowhere to run.

The rest of the visit was a blur (one of those out-of-body experiences that's akin to addressing thousands from notes you can't read, or bumping into a movie star in a public restroom), but I do know that I now had a target to attach my venom to—a real-live person whose voice I could remember and whom I could now imagine addressing my children. *My* children!

What followed were about two years of tension. And sometimes "tension" was putting it extremely mildly.

Carol: I remember our first meeting a bit differently. In my memory, we were dropping the kids off about two weeks into David and I dating, and as we pulled up into the driveway, the youngest said, "Hey, wanna meet my mom?"

As I thought, "No freakin' way!" and said, "Unnh . . . " she ran into the house and dragged her mom out by the hand. As reluctant as I was feeling, Jennifer seemed totally together and prepared for this. And friendly.

I have the feeling I stared at my shoes quite a bit.

My first thought about Jennifer was that she was so thin (damn her) and pretty (damn her again) and adult. I was twenty-one at the time and felt incredibly . . . well, *young*. But I had also gotten an earful from David in his post-divorce anger about her (in his opinion) shortcomings. It was very hard not to look at her and see *only* those terrible things.

Another early meeting that stands out in my memory is from our wedding day. We decided to have a very simple ceremony with a justice of the peace, just David and I and the kids. The youngest (then five) decided last minute she didn't want to wear the dress she had on, and Jennifer had to run over and bring another. I wanted to cry right alongside the five-year-old for having my special day ruined. But I had to be the grown-up.

When I met David, I fell for him hard and am more in love with him every day. Adding two stepkids and an ex-wife into the picture is certainly not what I had in mind when I was younger and pictured myself married with two kids.

Hmmmm . . .

If you were paying close attention, you might have noticed that we *each* have different memories about how and when we first met. How can this be? Obviously, someone's *wrong!*

Well, Jennifer doesn't remember meeting Carol in a car. And Carol doesn't remember ever coming over to Jennifer's house on David's motorcycle, so who's right? We don't know! But we left our differing versions of reality in to prove a point: There are often *miles* between the perspectives of stepmoms and moms. But each perspective is perfectly and completely valid, because it is true for THAT person and that person alone.

Let's take a closer look at what it's actually like to be a stepmother and mother who unwillingly have to deal with each other. Ironically, mothers and stepmothers have a lot more in common than they realize.

COMMON FEATURES OF THE STEPMOM/EX-WIFE LANDSCAPE

Not *all* stepmothers and ex-wives want to kill each other, but unfortunately, those pairs seem to be in the minority. Judging from our own experiences and stories told to us by others, most women in this situation do not get along. Here's what they're wrestling with:

- jealousy
- territoriality and competitiveness
- anger and resentment
- insecurity, anxiety, and outright fear

- grief, sadness, and despair
- helplessness and feeling overwhelmed
- denial and avoidance
- stress

Swallowing battery acid

Jealousy must be one of the worst feelings in the world. You feel smaller, stupider, and uglier in some fundamental way, not to mention . . . weaker. It's like a corrosive goop eating away at your insides. As you can see from our stories above, it came up for both of us, right away, and perhaps, if we're being honest, still rears its head occasionally to this day, in the tiniest of ways.

One thing that makes ex-wife/stepmother situations that much harder: It's easier to be jealous of someone you don't know that well. You end up projecting all sorts of things onto her. She's better than you at this or that. She seems to have or be something that you'll never be. Perhaps the other woman seems prettier, more successful, more organized, and more creative than you. She actually seems like she has her shit together, whereas you, well—you're all too aware of the parts of your life in need of emergency triage.

One hugely complicating factor is any jealousy that happens to be left over on the part of *the exes*. Usually, when a romantic relationship dissolves, one side is still left wishing it could have worked, while the other side is ready to walk away. This can throw a monkey wrench in the best laid plans for creating stepmother/mother harmony and we'll talk more about that later in this chapter.

Then there are all the various bonds and connections.

You may feel jealous of the relationship that the other woman has with the kids (whether they're hers or not). You may feel jealous if the stepmom has had kids with your ex. You may feel jealous of the history that your husband has with *his* ex. You may feel jealous of the new couple's happiness or standard of living. You may feel jealous of the freedom that the ex-wife now seems to have on the weekends, while you're watching *her* kids, or the freedom that the stepmom seems to have in her life when the kids aren't there.

The list goes on and on and unfortunately, it usually does. Jealousy leads smack-dab into our next emotions: territoriality and competitiveness.

This land is my land

What's our natural impulse when we feel threatened? We hunker down and devise a plan, or we get all fired up and fight for what we believe is rightfully ours.

When you feel *territorial,* you're hyper-aware of where the lines are and whether anyone's crossing them. Mothers often feel this way about "sharing" their children with a stranger. Stepmothers often feel this way about having their home periodically "invaded" by the step-kids, or having to change their parental rules because of how things are normally done "at home."

You're essentially saying here, "That's mine. And that, and that . . . and that too." Both women have their antennae up and tuned: Is the other person staying within her limits, or not? If anyone has the nerve to tangle with you, you feel energized and even more alert.

When you feel *competitive,* you want the other woman to understand once and for all that you are better than she is, you are the superior human being. You'll look for opportunities to make her look bad. What you're doing is *strategizing,* although that's probably not how you think of it in your head. There's the sense that if you slack off, you'll be overtaken. This all gives you plenty of combustible material for our next emotion.

Life-giving fire

If you're like most stepmoms and moms who've been thrown together, you probably get pissed off very easily at the other person. You may be uncomfortably familiar with the heat of your anger and resentments as they simmer on a daily, low flame, or occasionally rise to a full-on boil.

You may be doing your best to contain your anger, but find yourself accidentally snarling at innocent bystanders, like the kids or your partner. It doesn't make it any easier that your friends and family seem to stoke your anger either, helping you feel indignant and offended.

You might be loath to admit it, but sometimes you enjoy the power that goes along with feeling angry, not that we know (cough) anything about that. Carol used to continually feel like she had to bear the consequences of Jennifer's parenting mistakes. And Jennifer used to get continually mad at what she saw as parental micromanagement and interference on Carol's part.

If your ire consistently overtakes you, you may feel vengeful. You may *wish* you could see a way out of being so mad because it feels so terrible, but don't know how. And while anger is traditionally thought to be an emotion of passion and heat, you sometimes find that your anger makes you feel cold and unyielding. You go around in circles, because new things keep happening to feed the flames.

Which just makes you anxious . . . .

Please. Just. Stop.

You may feel buffeted by an ever-present anxiety and fear when it comes to the ex-wife or stepmother in your life, like ocean cliffs being pummeled by incessant waves. This comes from clashes over power, exposure, and control.

You may secretly worry that the other woman has something "over you." With the increased contact between the two family units, you often end up being privy to private details about each other, through tidbits that the kids bring back home or adult conversations. In the back of your mind, you know this *goes both ways,* which can make you feel naked and exposed. *What does she know about me that I wish she didn't? What vulnerabilities of mine have been revealed? How can I cover myself back up and protect myself?*

You may both feel that something that is rightfully yours, and yours only, has been taken away by the other woman. For stepmoms, it's often the sanctity of a new marriage and the chance to start off "fresh." For moms, it's usually someone else usurping a role that's always been hers as the mother figure. Both parties feel put *out* and put *upon.*

Jennifer hated knowing that Carol was learning all her dirty laundry from David, Carol's new husband (and Jennifer's ex). Carol couldn't stand having her carefully laid plans trumped by a last-minute change in plans from Jennifer.

Like it or not, women are typically the hands-on caregivers in our culture. Even if you're not the "motherly" type, as a stepmother you will likely be expected to fulfill the maternal role for your stepchildren. And the mother now has to share part of her parenting role with another woman. She is used to sharing her parenting with the father, but with another woman, no! Both sides have to share power with each other. Neither side asked for permission for that power. Neither side granted it. And yet there the arrangement lies.

These inescapable realities can simply grind both women down. If this strain continues too long unabated, both women may find themselves flagging.

Loss is part of nature

Both parties have something to grieve, and those feelings can run deep, deep, deep.

For the ex-wife, there's the sadness that comes from getting a divorce, no matter who initiated it. The marriage could not be saved, though one or both sides may have really tried. The "nest" could not be saved for the children. The parents could not be kept together. Now the kids will forever be going from house to house, splitting their worlds in two, never to be one, complete family again. No matter what was broken *inside* the marriage, most mothers still do not want for their children to have to live within the confines of a *broken family.*

For the stepmother, there is the sadness at starting out her marriage to a man she loved enough to marry without the luxury of a clean slate, *just the two of them.* She fell in love with *him,* aware that he was a package deal, but she probably, truly, had no idea what she was getting into. She has to share him with his children. She also has to try to form relationships with those same children, and this may or may not go well. There's the stereotype of the evil stepmother out there, setting people against her before she's even started. And she has to deal with his ex-wife and maybe even *her* husband or partner, too.

Both women have regrets about where they've ended up.

Carol still thinks that being a stepmom is one of the hardest things she's ever done. And Jennifer still regrets that divorce is a reality for her children.

Stepmoms and moms may have the sense that they just can't make things any better with the other. One may have tried at different times and been rebuffed. She may be tired of trying, or feels bruised and damaged.

The other woman may feel she's under siege and has to deal with someone who's, frankly, impossible.

For both women, there is the inescapable reality: *The other woman is here to stay.* And this fact only reinforces their continual feeling of despair.

Who pilfered my toolbox?

Having an ex-wife or stepmother in your life is like being stuck with a coworker you can't stand, on an important project where your ass is on the line. It's overwhelming, deflating, and maddening all at the same time! You can't *talk* to each other, you can't plan, and you don't collaborate. You're both already aware that the other person can't stand you.

Despite all these impediments, you still *have* to work together. So when things go wrong, as they inevitably do, they often do so spectacularly, like a plane going down in flames. All of which can lead to an anticipatory fatigue, a sense of predestined failure. Your sense of personal power feels inadequate and useless.

Even now that we get along (and have written a book together!), we still bump up against personality and style differences: totally opposing approaches to life and parenting. It's an ongoing dance . . . .

If you know that despite your best efforts, interactions with the other person are usually going to go wrong, it makes you want to avoid them altogether.

La-la-la-la, I can't hear you!

If you could never see the other woman again, you'd do it. If you could make it so that you never had to talk to her, hear her name in public, perhaps erase her from the face of the earth, you'd be the first one signing up.

As it is, you let someone else answer the phone if she's calling. You don't go outside when she picks up or drops off the kids. You do your best to pretend she doesn't exist.

Both of us used to use David as an intermediary so that we wouldn't have to interact with each other. It made life complicated, like we didn't speak the same language.

You may regularly have the sense that whatever's happening should not be happening. You may feel a strong sense of resistance and denial at the events unfolding in your life. You may feel victimized. You may be at a loss as to how any of this could possibly be your fault.

My stomach is eating itself

Put all these emotions together and you get *stress*.

It throws your life out of whack. It strains marriages, relationships with friends and family, and your body. It might be affecting your ability to relax, to focus, to concentrate, to enjoy yourself. We know we sure don't miss that feeling of a never-ending stream of problems with each other, making us irritable, tense, and depressed. And how nice not to have all those knots in our stomach anymore . . . .

So how does all of this play out in real life? Let's see this stuff in action!

MAXINE AND STEPHANIE DUKE IT OUT, FROM AFAR

Picture two women. Perhaps close in age, perhaps not. They both have similar duties, dealing with the maddening minutiae of running a household, tending to children or stepchildren, while working at a job. Their race, income, and educational level do not matter. Their lives share many similarities, but try telling them that!

Meet Maxine the ex-wife and Stephanie the stepmom. They take turns parenting two children, a ten-year-old boy named Michael and an eight-year-old girl named Courtney.

Maxine and Jeff are divorced, and clearly, Stephanie and Jeff are married. The children live with their mother, but go to their father's on Wednesdays and every other weekend.

What can we learn about the typical life of a mother and step-mother from a ten-minute snapshot of their lives?

Meet Stephanie the stepmom

Stephanie is at work. She's right in the middle of getting her notes together for a big project her boss has asked her to tackle (and she'd better not screw it up, either, this could lead to bigger and better things) when the phone rings.

It's Jeff. Could she pick up the kids today after school? His meeting has been moved up and now there's *absolutely no way* he can leave early to go pick up the kids from school. Michael's got another stomachache and Courtney is freaking out about getting home early to work on her science fair project.

Stephanie inwardly fumes. *It's due in two days, why wasn't Maxine helping her work on this thing before?* She imagines herself having to help a sullen and uncooperative Courtney later on this evening.

Stephanie is aware of her open cubicle. "Uh, actually no, honey. I can't. I've *got* to finish this stuff up."

Jeff's voice tightens with worry. He can't reach Maxine and his meeting is just about to start. The kids are waiting outside school and the buses have already left. He's in a bind.

"If there's *any* way," Jeff leaves the sentence unfinished, but Stepha-nie still feels the pressure. "Or . . . would you mind *terribly* trying to reach Maxine again to let her know what's happened?"

Stephanie sighs. The last thing she wants to do is have a conversa-tion with *her*. She goes to the break room for some privacy, takes a deep breath, and calls Maxine.

Nope, she can't do it either. And Maxine seems almost *happy* about this, eager to throw it back in Stephanie's lap. She's unwilling to budge even an inch and they're *her* children!

Fine, Stephanie's hand has been forced. Again. Now she'll have to ask her boss if she can leave for yet another family emergency.

But that's all right, because somehow, *some way,* she'll find a way to make Maxine *pay* for this. The next time she needs them to be flexible or cooperative about some change in the schedule, no such luck. Maybe then she'll have the opportunity to think twice about what a *flake* she is.

Meet Maxine the mom/ex-wife

Maxine has to drive up north yet again for work, the third time this week. Her car is going through gasoline like it was air. Luckily, the kids are going to Jeff's tonight and she can just focus on her errand, then getting home.

She has the sudden urge to check her cell phone. Sure enough, Jeff has called. Great, he needs her to pick up the kids again, he can't. Not only that, Courtney's crying and Michael threw up again. *(What IS going on with that kid lately? What is she feeding him?)* Stephanie can't leave work and he's already late for a meeting.

Well, why the hell didn't they figure this all out earlier? Maxine scowls as the highway traffic comes to a halt. And Stephanie is right there, less than a mile from the school. She can't go, my ass. She works at home one day a week and she can never seem to go pick them up then, either. How convenient.

Maxine's temper climbs even higher as she fumbles through her cell phone to dredge up Stephanie's number. She can't ever remember that stupid thing, it has no pattern to it.

Just then her phone rings. It's Stephanie's name on caller ID. Her innards contract.

"Jeff can't pick up the kids and I can't leave work." Stephanie's voice is flat and cold.

"Well, *I* certainly can't go. I'm stuck in traffic. It's not my day anyway."

There is a long pause. Did they get disconnected?

"Hello?" It's always impossible talking to this woman. "I said I can't make it either. I'm still on my way up—"

"*I* will go and get them then." Stephanie says this so dramatically, like she's the emperor making an official pronouncement.

Maxine straightens up in her seat. She's relieved, but still annoyed.

"Thanks, I appreciate it." (For crying out loud, *someone's* got to be the adult here.)

But she is talking to the air.

Stephanie has already hung up. *Without even saying goodbye! The nerve!* And she was going to *thank* her for picking up her own children? *Why should she thank her?* It was *Jeff's* responsibility anyway.

JOURNAL

Can you relate to any of the feelings or challenges that Stephanie and Maxine are struggling with? List three tangly emotions or situations you can identify with.

Gnarly feeling/challenge No. 1

_____

_____

_____

Gnarly feeling/challenge No. 2

_____

_____

_____

Gnarly feeling/challenge No. 3

_____

_____

_____

Circle the one that you're having the hardest time with. You'll have the opportunity to take a closer look at these feelings at the end of the chapter. We'll come back to Stephanie and Maxine later on in the book.

Right now, we'll switch our lens to a member of the male species for a little change in focus.

WHAT ABOUT THE MAN?

There may be two men in the picture if the ex-wife has a partner or is remarried, but for now, we're simply going to focus on the ex-husband and his potential impact on the relationship between the two women.

How he feels about things in this situation makes an enormous difference. He can be a positive influence or divisive. He may seem pitted against his ex-wife, or overly sympathetic toward her. He may be adding to conflict by gossiping about his ex with his wife, which is understandable but unhelpful. He may still be holding onto old hurts and resentments from his broken marriage.

Privacy

He may fear having the two women get along, because of how he imagines this might impact him. He may fear having all his secrets exposed.

In our situation, one of David's biggest fears was the possibility of us getting together and bitching about him. Sadly, his deepest fears were actually realized. Bonding over David's quirks has been at the top of our list of funny subjects for several years now. *But*—we make sure to *only* bitch about him in the most affectionate of ways—and he now knows that we *never* cross a certain line. He also knows that we *both* take care to preserve the sanctity of his marriage to Carol.

His own marriage

He may worry about the ex "tainting" his current marriage and screwing *that* all up. If things are already somewhat working in his relationship, he may fear that those successes are now going to be lost, too. One divorce was enough!

He may not want the ex-wife to insert herself into their lives any more than she already has, because her existence is already uncomfortable for them. She breaks the sense of their closed circle. She's an influence that *has* to be responded to because of the children, like it or not. It feels weird not having his romantic relationship be more private, like most people get to have when they first fall in love.

Jealousy

We mentioned jealousy earlier in this chapter, and it deserves another look here. If one person from the previous marriage is still attached to the other person, this is potentially going to cause some real complications. We've all experienced the pain of lopsided relationships where you have a grueling time letting your partner go. If this kind of dynamic plays itself out here, it can make it very difficult to proceed with a more cooperative relationship between the two women. The new wife will be rightfully wary of either inviting the ex-wife *in* to her life (if the ex-wife is still carrying a torch) or making sure to keep her *away* (if she senses that it's her husband who's still torn).

Carol said she had to get to know Jennifer better and see up close, for her own self, whether Jennifer seemed to be still in love with David. When Carol could see that she wasn't harboring any fantasies of getting back together with him, and when she felt assured that the same thing was true for David, *then* she felt safer becoming friends with Jennifer.

We can't tell you how to get over your ex, nor can we tell you what to do if you sense your husband is still emotionally incomplete with his ex. Those issues are a bit beyond our capabilities. However, there is still much to be gained from this book by increasing your understanding of the other woman's world.

Whatever the case, if the ex-husband/husband is supportive of the two women getting along, it helps pave the way for potential progress. Obviously, he can't *make* that happen either, if they are not inclined. If he's *against* them getting along, it's still possible, even without the women having to "go behind" his back.

He could even serve as a sort of "go-between" for both parties, broadcasting good intentions and buffering misunderstandings. That's what happened with us.

JOURNAL

Who initiated the divorce? What's the father's relationship like with the ex-wife? Does he still seem to have lots of old "baggage" in the form of complaints and hurt feelings? Is either of the exes still carrying a torch for their former spouse? Is the ex-wife paired up or single? What's his initial response to the idea of the two women getting along?

_____

_____

_____

_____

_____

_____

_____

_____

_____

_____

_____

_____

_____

_____

_____

_____

Answers to the questions above can help shed light on some of the underlying tensions in the relationship between the former partners and, by proxy, all the adults. We'll take a much closer look at the ex-husband/husband's influence in Chapter Two.

Now, let's examine some of the other factors that contribute to an adversarial relationship between stepmothers and mothers.

EXTERNAL INFLUENCES

Saving face

What's a powerful stimulant of the worse kind? Having an enemy in your life who's out to get you; someone who wants to reveal your weaknesses and mistakes; who aims to dominate and humiliate you. It keeps you on your guard and makes you feel subtly under constant attack. And strangely, it can also make you feel vaguely guilty and ashamed, as if you've already done something wrong, whether you have or not. We all want to be able to hold our heads up high and feel like we're still basically doing okay with what we have, even though we know our life will never be free of problems.

Carol remembers relishing secrets she knew Jennifer wouldn't want her to know. Jennifer remembers being frustrated by the fact that Carol seemed to remain an enigma—there wasn't anyone around who could fill her in on all the juicy details.

The game becomes about saving face and maintaining privacy. You want to gather dirt, to uncover the other person's secrets, her insecurities, her mistakes and fears, and *win*.

Understandable. But that means you're still playing the game, keeping it alive. And you're at risk, too.

Greenbacks

When it comes to money, one family is probably going to have more and the other family is probably going to have less. It should come as no surprise that the standard of living for mothers often goes down after a divorce. Women don't traditionally earn as much as men, even if they're doing the same job.

This inequity can make things extremely contentious between the two parties, because money hits us *where we live*. It triggers our survival instincts and often brings up very strong, core emotions, such as fear, anger, and the desire for revenge. Of course, there are state rules and guidelines in place to allocate spousal and child support, but even then, many divorced and recombined families are going to end up very unhappy about money.

Carol used to feel extremely frustrated about the child support payments that Jennifer received. She thought Jennifer didn't spend her money or manage her career the way Carol thought she should. And Jennifer could sense that Carol somehow resented the child support payments, even though she felt justified in receiving them as the full-time parent.

It's tricky. For the ex-husband and his new wife, it probably feels as if there's money flying out the window that should rightfully be staying in their house, even if the children live with their mom. For the ex-wife, she probably feels a bit screwed if her ex and his wife both work and make more money than she does.

Unless both parties get to the point where they feel like things are basically fair, or are willing to just let some things go, even if they're not fair, their perspective on money issues will likely influence how giving and flexible they are, how willing they are to create a connection between the two households.

The legal system, or speaking in tongues

When Jennifer and David were in the process of negotiating their divorce, they wanted it to be as amicable as possible. Yet once Jennifer received the divorce papers, the language seemed so adversarial and blaming. She felt as if David had "turned on her" somehow and gone against their original agreement, when really, that's just how those things are written.

The legal system often makes it seem like there's got to be a winner and a loser. If you find yourself getting more riled up after you read the legalese of your divorce or child custody documents, this may be one reason why. Many people find themselves getting sucked into lengthy, expensive court battles that are actually exacerbated by standard legal terms and phrases.

It doesn't help that you're often paying large sums of money, billed by the minute, to have someone craft unintelligible, legally binding documents for you in Mandarin Chinese, which only reinforces your sense of fear and helplessness.

Drama, or throw another log on the bonfire

How many sitcoms, movies, or books do we have that show us two split families getting along? Why is it so incredibly rare?

These two family units are not *expected* to get along, and when most people talk about these situations, they're bitching about each other. As a result, friends and family just think they're doing you a favor, bitching right alongside you . . . .

Not only that, there's a good chance they're already dead set against the other side before you even say anything. In a way, even if you *wanted* to approach the situation positively, it would be hard, going against the hate-chorus.

The two teams or family units are separate, different. There's one team with the ex-husband and the stepmom and their own version of reality, over there having pillow talks at night about the mom. And in her corner, the mom is doing the same thing with her partner or who-ever makes up her support system.

You know what it's like when you talk badly about someone, when you continually complain and vent and grumble. You see that person as opposed to you, *against* you, as the subtle (or maybe not so subtle) enemy. It makes it harder to reach out to each other and connect. Or forgive.

None of our friends or relatives ever thought we'd move past being typical adversaries. They just thought the existence of the other meant that we had a *huge,* unfortunate thorn in our sides to deal with. Our hands were tied. We were just going to have to wait it out and keep our fingers crossed that the other person would suddenly change from a bitch into someone who was at least bearable!

The sheer number of people involved in two split families is also pretty mind-scrambling and adds to the drama. Think about all the possible permutations for relationships of every single person to every-one else. Who would have thought you'd end up "related" to so many other people by getting divorced or married!

UNITED BY THEIR DIFFERENCES

Sure, the mother's and stepmother's desires, goals, and even lifestyles may be very different, but they've got one very important thing in common. Neither one of them is *ever* going to be the traditional "nuclear wife" in a nuclear family made up of Mom, Dad, and the little ones. Perhaps an acknowledgment of the challenges and heartache associated with this fact can be one of the first bridges built between them.

Quiz: Whose world Is this?

Let's take a look at the differences and similarities between these three situations. Read each sentence below and decide who this statement belongs to: Nuclear Mom (NM), Stepmom (SM), or Ex-wife (EX)?

Parental support from partner

_____ My parenting ideas clash with the way he's always done it.

_____ We may have different styles, but he's always been there as my backup.

_____ This is hard doing this mostly on my own now.

Financial security

_____ Our future would be a lot brighter if money weren't always flying out the window for child support.

_____ At least we're in it together, even if we're always struggling.

_____ Things feel pretty shaky, even with child support.

Priority of the romantic relationship

_____ I always feel like our relationship comes second, or worse. We never got a "fresh start."

_____ It may be rocky at times, but we know it's best for family stability if we put us first.

_____ I always feel torn between trying to give the kids enough attention and trying to find the space in my life to even have a relationship.

Bond with the children

_____ I sometimes feel a sense of mutual dislike between the kids and me. I also know they sometimes feel guilty for liking me.

_____ We've got the regular chaos of family life, but at least all of our connections are pretty straightforward.

_____ Being the full-time parent has actually made my relationship with the kids a little worse because I never have time to bounce back from disagreements.

Ability to plan for the future

_____ I never know if our plans will get screwed up by surprises from her or the kids.

_____ Sure, we've got bills, teenagers, and college to plan for, but at least we still have each other.

_____ It's scary to feel like it's all on my shoulders.

Possibility of additional children

_____ I wish we could decide this issue without always having to take the stepkids into consideration.

_____ Do we want more or not? Let's decide together whether this works for the whole family.

_____ Even though I'm remarried and we've had more, there's always this feeling of a "split" between the two sets of kids.

Relationships with extended family

_____ I now have three sets of extended families—not just the traditional two, but with his ex-wife and her relatives, too.

_____ We've got two to deal with, and that's enough, happy or not.

_____ I now have just one—I feel the loss of one whole side.

Sense of being in control of her life

_____ I am always aware of the fact that my desires may be trumped at any time by the kids or, worse, her.

_____ Regular life challenges throw me for a loop occasionally.

_____ I'm struggling to keep my head above water as a full-time parent while working.

What do you think? Some items seem to fit in other categories too, don't they? We're hoping that this quiz helped you see life through the other woman's eyes a little more clearly. Each situation has its own unique challenges and strengths.

Advice we can't give

There are some problems we can't address in this book because they're beyond the scope of our topic, *and* our expertise. Examples would include child abuse, substance and alcohol abuse, and truly crazy people (which is different from just being a bitch, trust us).

For those kinds of issues, you'll need to consult the help of a trained professional because we're not therapists, nor do we play one on TV. Even if finances are a factor, there are many free treatment options available if you're persistent and determined. Search around online. Make a few calls and ask for referrals. Ask friends for recommendations.

Even if it takes you some time, keep trying until you find a source of help.

EXTRA REASSURANCE

There's plenty of room in the boat

If you're feeling discouraged, just know that we're describing the worst of it. And if you're struggling, just know that this is exactly where you need to be, or at least, you're somewhere perfectly normal for this situation. You're not "doing it wrong" if you're having a hard time. Everyone else is in the same boat with you, so climb in and grab a seat.

There is a way to break through these feelings, though it may be hard to believe at the moment.

We know this because we've done it. We've grappled with all these negative feelings and situations ourselves, and over time, were able to move through them into something healthier and more positive. Now, we can actually *laugh* at some of those horrible memories, sympathize with the insecurities and fears of the other, and explain our once hostile and manipulative actions.

As we wrap up this section, we'd like you to get a more solid sense of the problems you're grappling with now, so that you'll know what you'd like to work on as you move through the book.

Quiz: Which geographical features do I recognize?

Filling out the section below will serve as your "before" snapshot. You'll have a chance to take an "after" picture too at the end of the book to see how much progress you've made. Now's your chance to let it all hang out. Where are you with the following difficult emotions?

On a scale of one to ten, rate this emotion as you experience it in specific situations and overall. If you need more room, feel free to write on a piece of paper (but make sure to hold onto it; you'll want to refer back to it later).

Jealousy	Overall intensity:	1 2 3 4 5 6 7 8 9 10	
With whom:	Intensity:	In what situation:	

Territoriality/ Competitiveness	Overall intensity:	1 2 3 4 5 6 7 8 9 10	
With whom:	Intensity:	In what situation:	

Anger and Resentment	Overall intensity:	1 2 3 4 5 6 7 8 9 10	
With whom:	Intensity:	In what situation:	

Insecurity and Fear	Overall intensity:	1 2 3 4 5 6 7 8 9 10	
With whom:	Intensity:	In what situation:	

Sadness and Despair	Overall intensity:	1 2 3 4 5 6 7 8 9 10	
With whom:	Intensity:	In what situation:	

Helplessness/ Overwhelmed	Overall intensity:	1 2 3 4 5 6 7 8 9 10	
With whom:	Intensity:	In what situation:	

Denial and Avoidance	Overall intensity:	1	2	3	4	5	6	7	8	9	10
With whom:	Intensity:			In what situation:							

Stress	Overall intensity:	1	2	3	4	5	6	7	8	9	10
With whom:	Intensity:			In what situation:							

JOURNAL

How'd you do? Which difficult emotion seems to be one of the biggest for you? You'll have an opportunity to tackle this in the next section.

_____

_____

_____

_____

_____

_____

_____

RESOURCES TO EXPLORE

Books

- *Ex-Etiquette for Parents: Good Behavior After a Divorce or Separation,* by Jann Blackstone-Ford and Sharyl Jupe
- *Stepwives: Ten Steps to Help Ex-Wives and Step-Mothers End the Struggle and Put the Kids First,* by Louise Oxhorn, Lynne Oxhorn-Ringwood, and Marjorie Krausz

- *Divorce Poison: Protecting the Parent-Child Bond from a Vindictive Ex,* by Richard A. Warshak

Web sites
- No One's the Bitch (www.noonesthebitch.com)
- Stepfamily Foundation (www.stepfamily.org/)
- The National Stepfamily Resource Center (www.stepfamilies .info)

AS WE LEAVE THE CHAPTER

There's a certain comfort and security to be had in getting the lay of the land, in looking chaos squarely in the face. It helps you know what you're up against, how to plan for the future, how to figure out a strategy for getting somewhere better. And that's where we're heading, somewhere more hopeful, with lots more possibilities.

We've taken a look at what this strange, new, divorced and step-family territory looks like, with a pair of binoculars and, in a few places, a magnifying glass. Next, we're going to dive even deeper into murky water in our aim for clarity. Sound counterintuitive? Just imagine a mucky underwater tunnel, and at the very end, a crystal clear pond in the middle of a lush forest. We've got to do some spelunking first, but we'll be in that oasis soon.

2

Own Your Own Crap

(What, Me? A Dark Side?)

TURNING THE FLASHLIGHT ON

*Things were looking pretty bad the last chapter, huh? If you were taking a good look around the Stepmother/Mother landscape hoping to find reasons to feel **better** about your situation, you might not be too excited about **this** chapter. That's because we're going to be lifting up rocks to take a peek at things that might be hiding underneath. We might even poke at a few things! And we daresay, by the **middle** of this section, you could even be feeling some mighty strong resistance.*

But resistance is good!

Resistance would mean we're getting somewhere.

Resistance means there's a block in the dam. What happens when you remove the log, the rock, the collection of trash?

Voila!

The river flows, the pond or lake is replenished, all the birds start singing and the sun comes out, and Bambi delicately makes his way to the brook for a silent little sip.

But we're getting ahead of ourselves . . . .

A LOOK BACK FROM US

First, we're going to dredge up all of *our* yucky stuff. Okay, maybe not all, because that would require another book. But just so you know you're in good company, here's some of the gunk *we* used to live with on a daily basis.

Resentments

Carol: I resented the fact that Jennifer got so much of our money. There, I said it. It's always been a tough one for me, even before I started making money with my art, because David and I were in a *partnership*. Plus, I was working so hard to get my art career off the ground all the time. It was *really* hard to see her make the financial decisions she did, when part of what she was using was the money we gave her *for the kids*. And then when she asked us for more, for camps or whatnot. Oh my god, that really got me.

Jennifer: I resented the fact that Carol got to stay home, while I had to raise both of the girls full time *and* work to support us. It was exhausting and stressful and sometimes even scary. I used to judge Carol as having it pretty easy, with a husband to support her and plenty of money, and not much else to do except take care of the house and piddle around with her art. It really grated on me that the child support was supposed to cover *everything* extra, when we were sometimes just barely scraping by. I sometimes blamed Carol for that.

Comments from friends and family

Carol: With anyone I met, the words "my husband's ex-wife" generally produced a grunt, accompanied by a look of sympathetic understanding (that the ex is always a pain in the ass). That's the expectation. If you think about it, most divorces probably aren't the happiest of experiences, especially when kids are involved. And then throw money into the mix (child support and possibly alimony) and you've got a seriously volatile situation. No mom is going to be happy about the new wife-y when there are kids involved, so ex-wives usually equal trouble. I pretty much got that same reaction from all my friends, at least the few who were still willing to accept me after I married into such a crazy situation.

Jennifer: I got the same automatic, negative reactions. Friends and family were *more* than willing to be indignant with me about having to deal with a stepmom. Everyone I knew thought the same thing—a stepmother just tries to elbow her way into a situation where she doesn't belong. Why should she be surprised if she meets with resistance from the kids? I had lots of judgments about Carol's age (she was fourteen years younger) and her experience with life. In my mind, she was "playing house" with my children, and *they were not toys.*

How do I compare myself to thee?

Carol: Ways I compared myself to Jennifer? My boobs were smaller. My butt was bigger. Unfortunately, I got to hear all about the problems she and David had when they were married. I felt superior to her—I got to hear it all and she didn't have a clue about me. I also heard that she didn't like to do housework and that she rarely cooked. So I used to feel superior about that, too. If you've been to my house lately, you know why I don't anymore.

Jennifer: Carol always just seemed like such a domestic diva compared to me. It seemed as if she was always doing some cool art project with the kids or cooking interesting meals or whipping up beautiful hand-made holiday decorations. I sometimes felt so *old* next to her; her face is so fresh and unlined, she looks great even without makeup. She was intensely disciplined with her art, almost ruthlessly so, and I felt so unproductive compared to her. But whenever I figured out some of her insecurities, I would gloat.

Parenting wars

Carol: And then there was the parenting. I really judged Jennifer for that, I have to admit. I remember talking to her once on the phone and suggesting that she just lay down the law for misbehavior or impose consequences. And she just said, "But that just seems so *mean.*" And I thought she was being such a weenie, and hurting the kids in the process.

And every time the youngest child was upset, which seemed to be a lot in the beginning, she would say, "I want my mommy!" over and over and over and over. It would make me feel so useless and so left out and so disliked. She said that until she was about eight.

Jennifer: We had huge differences of opinion when it came to parenting. I saw Carol as being an unnecessary hard-ass, who expected submission and obedience just because she was the adult, not because her ideas were actually helpful or right. I saw her as coming from a place of fear and ego. But I was also jealous of her organized approach to parenting and discipline and felt inadequate, compared to all her charts and clear consequences for misbehavior. It took me a long time to see that the best approach was actually a *balance* of our two parenting styles: having the *structure* and the *nurturing*.

I was also jealous of her ability to actually work on various creative projects with the girls, because I never seemed to have the time or patience to do the same thing. And I sometimes felt smug, knowing that she was struggling, and the girls would always prefer me as their mother.

DISOWNING YOUR RELATIVES

How easy is it to transform a difficult situation if the problems are mostly "someone else's fault"? Not very. And why is that?

Because you put all the control in the other person's hands. In truth, though, you have just as much power as the other person does when it comes to shaping your own inner reality—if not way-y-y-y more. Here's where you're going to be ruthlessly honest about all the baggage *you're* bringing to the table—your role in keeping the conflict and score-keeping going. We're going to unzip your bags, dump everything out on the table, and examine what's traditionally called our *shadow selves*.

Shadow, meaning the darker parts of you. Shadow, as in something lurking behind you, or just off to the side, not usually within your field of vision.

One very important thing about our shadow sides: They're normally the parts of ourselves that we've disowned, like unwanted relatives. We don't want to admit they exist. We're ashamed of them; afraid, confused and befuddled, disgusted. We'd rather put our hand in a vat of acid and keep it there than put our arms around our shadows. But having the courage *and the curiosity* to face your shadows is the key to all kinds of freedom, not only in an ex-wife/stepmother relationship, but in all areas of your life.

Humility's surprise

Good ol' Carl Jung, who originated the shadow concept, once said that our shadow self "is that which we think we are not." So what does it look like in action? Luckily, the answer to this is easy: You deal with it almost every day. All you have to do is think about the people that you interact with on a regular basis. Just look to others and how they live.

The coworker who prides herself on being so fair and non-gossipy, but in private, rips colleagues to shreds. The friend who absolutely cannot *stand* it when people act smug and superior, yet is doing the *exact same thing* when she dissects their behavior. The stepmother who *swears* she's doing everything she can to get along better with the stepchildren, while in actuality, she bristles around them because she's truly *annoyed* by them. Or perhaps the mother who dramatically claims to love and adore her children so much, but is always trying to pawn them off on you for an extra child-free weekend.

Ironically, being willing to make yourself *smaller* and more humble will actually help you become bigger (in the best possible way) . . . and *stronger.* In this chapter we'll gently help you take stock of the cobwebs in your corners in preparation for creating a nice, sparkling, shiny house.

Three tricky monkeys

As you've probably already figured out, one telling characteristic of our shadow self is blindness and denial. As much as we'd like to think we're aware of our good sides and "bad," there are still aspects of ourselves that we're woefully unaware of.

Think back to all the examples given above. Another thing they have in common is transparency. The people doing their shadow thing above think no one can see what they're doing. But we can.

The examples above also have *projection,* or mirroring, in common. We often home in on the one thing we cannot stand in ourselves in other people. Then we "catch" them doing it and nail them for it (even if only internally). Their behavior gets under our skin. We feel indignant, contemptuous, and unforgiving.

Unfortunately, no one is above living from this place in themselves. Not you. Not the writers of self-help books. Not the Pope or the Dalai Lama. Even today, you probably did something that you think you really didn't.

What's our motivation for living in such an unattractive and unproductive way? We're sure you can see this one coming too . . . *protection* (or the illusion of it). We're doing our best to protect ourselves from unsavory aspects we'd rather not see.

Enough hiding. While our shadow sides might seem as threatening as snakes, remember, they're *your* snakes! You raised them. You fed them. Don't be afraid. You're actually immune to their venom, once you bring them out into the light of day.

We'll be uncovering them *together.* And we'll be doing so because it's one of the main ways to resolve conflict, though at first glance it may seem weird and unpleasant.

When you hold up your bucketful of serpents at the end of this chapter and proudly proclaim, "These are *mine!*" you're on the way to happier times.

The importance of + and -

Before we dive in, let's create a bit of deeper meaning to carry with us along the way. Sometimes we forget why it even matters if you get along with the stepmom or ex-wife in your life. It's like thinking of exercising when you're lying in bed, all warm and cozy. It's cold and weirdly dark outside, and you just suffered through one of the worst bouts of insomnia of your life. Why try so hard? Who cares? What difference will it make to the world if you just stay in bed?

Well, it all comes down to two little symbols: + and -.

Let's explain this with a chart:

(-)	(+)
misery	happiness
repetition	peace
chaos	contentment

In one corner, there's all that crap that usually attends these ex-/ step relationships. On the other side is what it would feel like if both you and the other woman were actually nice to each other most of the time.

The sad thing here is, if you just settle for --- (that's a big dose of the negative, for emphasis), you'll never know how good + could be. For example, if perhaps you began to make amends and focus on the desires you have in common, like making it easier for the kids to go back and forth between houses. Or keep better track of details that are forever getting lost in the shuffle.

Still feeling resistant to the possibility?

Well then, let's just revel in some forbidden feelings first! Does this book have to be chock-full of boulders to be rolled uphill? Who are we kidding? That gets *old*.

Let's look instead at why we should let just the rocks roll back down the hill and take a well-deserved break. See if you can relate . . . .

TOP TEN REASONS NOT TO EVEN BOTHER TRYING TO GET ALONG WITH THE STEPMOM OR EX-WIFE

Place a checkmark beside every statement that makes you nod your head in vigorous agreement.

_____ 1. She already hates me, there's no changing her. I'm sure she's stabbing me in the back right now!

_____ 2. If it weren't for her, I'd/we'd have a lot more money.

_____ 3. She's such a terrible step/mother. Just look at the way she
_____. (fill in the blank)

_____ 4. It's too hard, scary, weird, _____. (fill in
the blank)

_____ 5. She's such a control freak, meeting her halfway would be
hopeless.

_____ 6. She totally micromanages his relationship with his own
kids!

_____ 7. If I actually *tried* to get along with her, I'd just be letting
her off the hook for everything she's done in the past.

_____ 8. Don't I have enough on my plate without adding this to
the list?

_____ 9. You mean getting along is even *possible?* Are you out of
your mind?

_____ 10. Face it. This woman really *is* a bitch!

Feel better? You have to admit, there's a certain pleasure in just
giving in to this stuff, isn't there? What's ironic here is that *both* mothers and stepmothers feel like the above statements are true for them.
Both!

Okay, back to reality, but *pay attention.* This is where it gets juicy.

SHADOW SELF, UP CLOSE

Next, we'll be breaking down the specific ways our shadow sides mani-
fest themselves.

Sitting all alone in the bullet list below, each aspect of your dark side
might look harmless enough. But these traits have a powerful impact on
your life, even though they seem easy enough to ignore. These types of
behavior, and the thoughts and feelings that go along with them, are the
fuel that feeds the fires of conflict. They're what keep us invested in being
on the other side of the fence, in staying separate. They keep us locked in
a perpetual struggle with others, even people we really care about.

We hope you'll be pleasantly surprised by how many of these
elements actually fit you, instead of dismayed. Recognizing them in

yourself means you're that much closer to a breakthrough. Let's see if any these sound (uncomfortably) unfamiliar:

- Wanting to be right
- Wanting to "look good"
- Wanting to be superior
- Wanting to control others
- Playing the victim
- Giving in to insanity
- Shading the truth

Being right

Remember how good it feels to be right? To correctly predict someone's behavior, or its results? To watch someone else make a mistake that you wisely managed to avoid? To have just the right piece of obscure information that applies to a situation, magically fixing everything? A lot of us will go through amazing gymnastic contortions in order to be right . . . or at least *seem* right.

But when we look at this behavior from others' points of view—when we remember how it feels to have these things done to us—we find that it's annoying to be around people who are acting this way. When someone acts like a rigid know-it-all, we just can't stand it. But we also really like being right, don't we? Just about as much as we like looking good.

Wanting to "look good"

Most of us care about how we seem to others, especially family or close friends. But also people at work, our neighbors, casual acquaintances, even people we'll never see again at a store. We all have a built-in radar that monitors how we think we're coming across. We're used to a certain level of pride and a certain level of insecurity. If the levels dip down one way or fly up the other, we either consider ourselves to be having an "off" day or a great day. Basically, we know what we're used to.

But what happens when an enemy arrives on the scene? When we find a villain in our midst: someone who seems to be looking for cracks in our armor, or running mascara, or mistakes that we'd rather keep to ourselves? It's hard to relax when you know someone is just *waiting* for you to mess up—when you know that person is talking about you, watching you, biding her time.

The anxiety of wanting to look good lurks beneath a combative streak that can only be attributed to our next aspect of the shadow self.

Wanting to be superior

Whereas wanting to look good is all about having others approve of you, trying to win the dominance game is more about making others look *bad*. Feeling superior is pretty heady stuff. It can feel like you've finally made it to the top of the heap. You're the *man* (or the *woman*). You can survey your little kingdom up there amongst the clouds and gusts of wind, but . . . you can also fall down.

You're not too grounded when you're up there, feeling better than everyone else. Part of you knows that it's temporary, so you're compelled to constantly watch your back. Is anyone else attempting to clamber up your hill?

Which leads to your next shadow side, plotting and planning.

Wanting to be in control

This is you wanting to be in charge, playing your cards so that you're always coming from a strategically strong position. You do what you can to detect your opponent's weaknesses and insecurities. You play dead, if that works, or move forward quickly to throw someone off her balance. You manipulate details, events, and aspects of your life to try to gain the upper hand. You may find yourself playing out imaginary scenarios where you win and the other woman is humiliated, or finally and rightfully put in her place.

But as we all know too well, it's not nice for women to seem too power-hungry. We've got names for women like that (part of the title of this book, for one), so you may have to be sneaky. If being intense and hard-charging isn't your style, then the next aspect might be more appealing.

Power through victimhood

Cue the violins . . . . It's so hard when life is out to get you, isn't it? Some people just seem to have all the bad luck. And what makes it even worse is if you're *really trying*. You're a *good* person . . . and even when that "other woman" is coming after you like a dark figure on a horse, you still try to be nice. Fair. The sane, calm one. And where does it get you?

Screwed, that's what! Taken advantage of, left and right.

How's that for fairness?

Being the victim has its own kind of power, though. You get to be blameless. You're never the one doing anything "wrong." You're throwing up your hands and shaking your head when the broken lamp is discovered, essentially saying, "I didn't do it! And when have I *ever*?"

Remember the phrase "passive-aggressive"? It goes right along with being a victim. Passive-aggressive people have a conscious awareness of what they're doing when they, oops, "helplessly" arrange the situation so that the person in charge falls flat on his or her face. The victim ends up the victor or at least driving the more outwardly authoritarian person mad.

Which brings us to our next element.

Giving in to insanity

There's a kind of crazy aggression that comes out when we feel severely threatened. We'll do things we never thought we would, such as break into someone's e-mail account "because we had to." We'll go to great lengths to set someone else up to fail and severely stress ourselves out in the process. We'll lash out in some way and scare even ourselves.

When you're operating from this place, you feel justified in wildly attacking because you think you're being wildly attacked. But you are also not really in control. And your outrageous, uncharacteristic behavior is only inflaming the situation and making it harder to think straight and calm down.

Thinking straighter would probably head off the next shadow side.

"Shading" the truth

It was only a little white lie, we think. Or maybe just something you kept to yourself that you should have revealed. There's outright, planned deceit. And then there are the lies you twist around when you're caught, so that everyone ends up confused.

However you do it, it's just one more way to try to gain control, to try to make things go the way you want them to.

There's only one problem with this. You're working with faulty material. It's like shooting bullets from a gun with a bent barrel.

Lies have a way of getting away from you, taking on a life of their own. It's scary trying to keep track of lies, and sadly, they seem to have no expiration date. Plus, somewhere inside, you still feel guilty for lying (that's your conscience, trying to help you).

It may be inconvenient as hell to tell the truth. And you may temporarily feel at a disadvantage doing so, but you'll end up feeling more grounded and guilt-free.

Own your own shit!

So tell yourself the truth. Which shadow side traits have you dabbled in? What are some of your favorites? Which ones are making you think, hmmm, that might be interesting to try on for size? Put a check next to all that apply.

_____ Wanting to be right

_____ Wanting to "look good"

_____ Wanting to be superior

_____ Wanting to control others

_____ Playing the victim

_____ Giving in to insanity

_____ Shading the truth

By now, hopefully, you're starting to realize how much seemingly excusable, "perfectly understandable" behavior contributes to the problems you have with "the other woman."

One of the keys to improving your relationship with her is owning your own shit. You've got to claim what's yours. You know, admitting to the parts of you that help keep things cantankerous and conflict-ridden. You took your first steps by checking off any of the traits above. Good for you!

Part of you may still be saying, *surely,* this current state of affairs is *all her fault!* Are you starting to realize the possibilities for change if they're not?

Quiz: The joy of being judgmental

We invite you to take a close-up look at the "hamster wheel" in your brain that's constantly churning out unhelpful thoughts. Circle a number for each phrase. Be ruthlessly honest.

Rating Scale

1) No, I swear.
2) Maybe a smidgeon.
3) Okay, fine, yes.
4) Most definitely.
5) Dear God, I can barely stand how I feel.

1   2   3   4   5
I find myself critiquing her clothes.

1   2   3   4   5
I find myself critiquing her job (or lack of it).

1   2   3   4   5
I find myself critiquing her intelligence or education (or lack of it).

1   2   3   4   5
I find myself critiquing her personality (or lack of it) and mannerisms.

1   2   3   4   5
I find myself critiquing her friends, family, and social status.

1   2   3   4   5

I find myself critiquing her looks.

1   2   3   4   5

I find myself critiquing her taste in music, movies, books, cultural knowledge.

1   2   3   4   5

I find myself critiquing her housekeeping skills (or lack thereof).

1   2   3   4   5

I find myself critiquing her parenting skills (or again, lack thereof).

1   2   3   4   5

I find myself critiquing the way she handles money.

1   2   3   4   5

I find myself critiquing her current and past romantic relationships.

1   2   3   4   5

Her emotional blind spots are, like, so obvious to me!

Interpreting your score

- If you scored between 1–25 points: Congratulations, you're a saint! Please write to us and help us. We need you.
- If you scored between 26–50 points: Welcome to the human race! You're not doing so-o-o badly, but please keep reading.
- If you scored between 51–70 points: It's hot down here, isn't it? Use this book to fan yourself, then please, by all means, keep reading.

JOURNAL
What do you think about your results?

_____

_____

_____

_____

What would you like to change?

_____

_____

_____

_____

Compassion: the shadow is your friend!
It's best to try to approach your psychological explorations with compassion for yourself, instead of a critical eye, which is how we're used to approaching potentially difficult emotions. While it may not be comfortable looking at these issues, understanding *what* you're doing, *how* you're doing it—and *why*—is the key to moving closer to a sense of partnership between all of the adults.

Sure, we realize you're probably reading a lot of these paragraphs and going, "See? I knew that woman was up to no good. And now I can prove it!"

But we hope you're also reading and going "Hmmm... do I *ever* do this? Does this sound familiar, not only because *she* does it but because *I* do too?"

If you find yourself constantly answering a quick and vehement "no" to that question, go back and reread the part about projection.

What are you willing to own here?

To accept as yours, no matter how unflattering?

You're the only person reading this book right now; no one else is listening to the dialogue in your head. If you can't be honest with yourself now, when can you ever be?

The point is not to feel even worse because of your actions, or even angrier and more offended about the other woman's actions.

The point here is education, learning, *change*.

WHAT ABOUT THE MAN?

Is the husband/ex-husband feeding into any drama, or helping it heal? There are loaded concerns that both sides have in common, and concerns that are particular to just one "team." Let's break these into two camps for greater clarity.

Dynamics of the stepmother/ex-husband relationship

It's hard for the stepmom to start off with a "clean slate" with the mom. They almost always begin as adversaries because of the conflict involved in the divorce. Gossip and "processing" between the husband and wife can contribute to ongoing drama and create new conflict. They may have an agreed-upon story about why: he got a divorce and what was his fault—or where he was blameless; what kind of woman the ex-wife is; how things are probably going to go from here on out. He may be keeping different parts of his version of history alive, such as the victim, wronged party, better parent, etc., and a lot of negative feelings probably go along with that negative interpretation.

The husband may not want his wife to know or see the truth about some of the problems he had before with his ex-wife. He may secretly worry that these same issues will be a factor later on in his current marriage.

His unresolved baggage with his ex-wife can create communication problems between not only himself and his ex-wife but between all the adults too. There may be a lack of cooperation and inflexibility, power struggles, and one-upmanship.

JOURNAL

Stepmoms: What's your repeating loop of a "story" for your husband (victim, wronged party, better parent, etc.) that helps keep your negative emotions alive?

_____

_____

_____

_____

_____

_____

_____

_____

_____

_____

In your opinion, what's his?

_____

_____

_____

_____

_____

Do they match up? If not, how are they different?

_____

_____

_____

_____

_____

Dynamics of the ex-wife/ex-husband relationship

The ex-wife may feel like the other side is teaming up against her, two-to-one. She probably feels like the stepmother knows all her dirty laundry, but not, unfortunately, vice versa. She lacks someone to give *her* the inside scoop about the other woman, so she's in the dark.

There's a very good chance that she's got plenty of her own unresolved baggage with her ex-husband too, such as guilt, regret, sadness, and anger. And just like with her ex-husband, that leftover baggage makes it hard to communicate clearly, work together from a place of mutual support and cooperation, and move forward.

She may have lots to say when it comes to the flaws and shortcomings of her previous partner. But she's well aware that the other woman either does not see these (yet) or isn't bothered by them.

JOURNAL

Moms: What's your repeating loop of a "story" (victim, wronged party, better parent, etc.) that keeps your negative emotions alive?

_____
_____
_____
_____
_____
_____
_____
_____

In your opinion, what's your ex-husband's?

_____
_____
_____
_____
_____
_____
_____

How are they different? How do they fuel each other?

_____
_____
_____
_____
_____

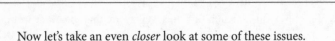

Now let's take an even *closer* look at some of these issues.

Holding a grudge

We all have our treasured stories, our old war wounds; the ones we repeat over and over inside our heads, bitterly listing the ways we've been done wrong. Every time you regurgitate your tale of woe about your ex-husband, or you egg your husband on about *her* offenses, you get a little hit of self-righteousness, a flash of indignation, and the pot starts to simmer all over again. Keeping your resentments alive can feel really good, though people are loathe to admit it.

What's even better is when a new juicy event takes place and now you *know* the other person has been proven to be a real jerk. You get to feel superior, to pull up the warm blanket of victimhood around your neck (or help your husband do it) and hunker down.

But think about it: How is doing this *really* helping you? How does harboring long-standing grievances and resentments ever get you anywhere? You're the one who's suffering.

For moms: What grudges are you still holding? How does this continued spite affect you? What would you like to do differently?

For stepmoms: What negative version of your husband's story are you helping to keep alive? How does this continued spite affect you? What would you like to do differently?

_____

_____

_____

_____

_____

_____

_____

_____

Trying to win the Better Parent award

For moms, you do whatever you can to set your ex-husband up to fail. Maybe you withhold information from him, like for sporting events or the children's playdates. Maybe you don't tell him about birthday parties or school events until the last minute so he can't come (and looks like he doesn't care, whereas, obviously, you *so* do). Worst of all, you may find yourself making little digs out loud with your own children. "Well, you were ready to go, it's your father who's late. As usual . . . ."

For stepmoms, you find yourself jumping through hoops trying to show your husband that you're a better mother figure than the children's mother. You're all too aware of her shortcomings after getting an earful from him. And you bend over backward doing things you're normally not that inclined to do, like arts and crafts or baking three-layer cakes, or fixing a bicycle or shooting hoops. It's a strain on you, doing these things, but you feel driven so that you can finally get those magical words of acknowledgment, "Wow, I wish I'd married you from the beginning."

For moms: Do you put a lot of effort into making your ex-husband look bad and yourself look better? Do you sometimes feel like you're screwing yourself with your schemes and intrigues?

_____

_____

_____

_____

_____

For stepmoms: Do you put a lot of effort into getting your husband to notice what a better mother figure you are? Do you sometimes feel like you're screwing yourself with your schemes and intrigues?

_____

_____

_____

_____

_____

_____

Being at the mercy of core issues

Sure, everyone loves talking about sex, but the second most important volatile issue has got to be money. Money gets us where it counts: in that core place of fear connected to matters of survival and our sense of power in the world. If you're keeping the fires of conflict stoked over issues of money, it actually might not be worth it. Can you attach a dollar figure to your angst?

When a family dissolves and becomes two separate units, one side is almost always going to have less. Unfortunately, given the way our culture works, that side is usually the ex-wife's.

Let's say every summer you argue with your ex-husband over whether he'll chip in some extra money for summer activities for your children, and he balks. You end up mad at him for months afterward, getting a few headaches here and there, snapping at the kids, dreading having to interact with him over the phone. Maybe it ruins a few evenings or weekends.

Or perhaps you and your husband go round and round about something expensive he wants to buy for the stepkids that he bought without asking you. You want to save money for *your* family, you want to make decisions *together*. You think he's acting out of guilt or is letting himself be manipulated by the kids, and you can't think about the whole thing without steam coming out of your ears.

For stepmoms: Put that cumulative stress into a bucket and ask yourself: Is all of this worth an argument over $_____ (insert dollar amount here)? What are your thoughts on this?

_____

_____

_____

_____

_____

_____

_____

For moms: Put that cumulative stress into a bucket and ask yourself: Is all of this worth an argument over $_____ (insert dollar amount here)? What are your thoughts on this?

_____

_____

_____

_____

_____

_____

_____

Denying the what-if fantasies

As we mentioned before, if one person is not completely "done" with the relationship, it adds a whole new combustible element to the situation. Even if the ex-wife is complete with the end of her marriage, it may still feel odd to see another woman in her "role."

We think these kind of lingering feelings are perfectly normal, and yet, they're squirmy for even *us* to talk about, perhaps *especially* for us to talk about! Despite whatever negativity you might feel toward your ex, there's always the chance that a strong attachment to him is still lurking *somewhere* in your energetic field. After all, you had children together! You shared your lives in the most intimate of ways.

Jennifer: I remember several years after we'd split up, being occasionally haunted by dreams where my ex and I were still together, perhaps exploring a new house we were soon to move into, or taking a family trip to strange environs. Waking up from those dreams always left me disoriented and slightly embarrassed: Now what was THAT all about? Did this mean I still wanted to be with him? Or that we were somehow meant to be? Even now that he was remarried, and I was dating someone else? I would always come back to the same answer: This is the life we have now, and he and I seem happier . . . .

These types of dreams and mental wanderings are perfectly natural; not only that, they are commonplace. What's the old saying? The more you struggle to be free of something, the more you're reinforcing the fact that there's still a need to struggle? If you've got some hallucinatory misfits bumbling around in your psyche, just know you're not alone. Perhaps a lot of these feeling are biologically motivated; a part of you simply wants to put the two halves of a circle back together. If you find yourself actively trying to undermine your ex's new marriage, or having difficulty creating new relationships, get some professional help. Otherwise, these feelings will likely fade with time.

For moms: Have you ever submerged any what-ifs? If you are aware of these feelings inside of you, are you okay with them, or struggling?

_____

_____

_____

_____

_____

_____

_____

_____

_____

For stepmoms: Do you worry that your husband might still have feelings for his ex-wife? If you are aware of these feelings inside of you, are you okay with them, or struggling?

_____

_____

_____

_____

_____

_____

_____

_____

DUDE, WHERE'S MY TROPHY?

Are you waiting for that arbitrary moment in time when all the chips will be tallied and a winner will be declared in the Worthiness and Goodness of Being a Human Being contest?

We don't know why this is, but human beings often live in an odd state of limbo, lives subtly on hold. It's like we're still little kids waiting for an authority figure in the guise of someone we look up to, or an internalized version of God, to finally give us that one, all-important stamp of approval, showing once and for all that not only are we just fine but, fingers crossed, we're actually superior. We're waiting for that big day when we get a ribbon pinned to our shirts or a trophy handed to us onstage to thunderous applause, or perhaps just to be lauded by countless glowing articles in major newspapers around the country.

Probably ain't gonna happen.

The only thing to do if you recognize this dynamic in yourself is to just give up. Decide to stop waiting. Not. One. More. Day. You do this by accepting complete responsibility for creating your own life (more on this later in Chapter Four), which, at the moment, may sound about as appealing as carrying an extra bag of sand over the mountain. But there's a good reason to take on that extra weight. Read on.

EMOTIONAL MATH: PAYOFFS VS. COSTS

Managing you

So how does this all balance out with our dark side? Can't we just live this way and get away with it? Isn't this what most of us are doing anyway? Especially in these ex-wife/stepmother situations, where there's so much awkwardness, so much anger, so much miscommunication. How are you supposed to fix all that when you have no control over the other person?

Well, right now, we're not talking about controlling *her;* we're talking about you managing . . . *you.*

One concept that might motivate you to make some changes is to consider the costs and payoffs, or benefits, for your behavior. When you unconsciously act from your dark side, it takes something away from your life. You think it's worth it, but we beg to differ.

The payoffs always *seem* so big when you're right in the middle of this stuff, but the costs are usually *huge.* And we don't usually attribute the costs directly to our behavior. We find some type of circular reasoning to weasel our way out of a direct connection.

Benefits

Here are some typical payoffs, or strokes for our all sneakiness, our resentments, our manipulations and judgments. We:

- Feel superior, smarter
- Feel self-righteous
- Get sympathy from others
- Feel like we're getting a good look inside the other person—we can wisely see what she can't
- Feel like we're gaining a strategic advantage
- Feel innocent and "good"
- Get to relax—there's nothing for us to do or change because it's not our fault!
- Get to feel in control of our life by comparing someone else's obviously "unconscious," blind actions to ours
- Get validating anger and indignation from others

Some additional benefits to feeling like a victim (the ones above still apply):

- We're wronged, the injured party.
- We feel entitled to compensation of some kind.
- We get reinforcement of our crappy self-image (the comfort and safety of the known environment, even if it's lousy).
- The "safety" of not having failed.
- The safety of not having been proven a "loser" through your own actions—someone else's actions are at fault.

Costs

And what are the costs? They can affect almost every area of your life. From your general level of happiness and stress, to your marriage, your health, and your relationship with your kids (especially your relationship with your kids!). Here's what's happening when you keep playing this stuff out over and over in your head:

- We feel stressed.
- We're unhappy.
- We feel an overall sense of not being able to relax, to be at peace.
- We snap at others or get easily irritated.
- Our hearts feel hardened, even when we want them to soften up.
- We feel overwhelmed by our mental self-talk and don't know how to make it stop.
- We get headaches, stomaches, and maybe get colds more frequently.
- We pay less direct attention to our children.
- We have less energy to play with them or a reduced ability to connect with them.
- We bore our friends and family with all our complaints and gossip and need to "vent" and process our broken-record feelings.

- We feel sad and don't know why.
- Our innards feel hard with anger and resentment.
- We cannot forgive others as easily as we wish we could, or know we should, in moments of clarity.
- We miss opportunities to make things better.

We could go on. But we think you get the idea.

What benefits or payoffs for negative emotions can you relate to?

_____

_____

_____

_____

_____

_____

How are these benefits costing you? What are the consequences in your life?

_____

_____

_____

_____

_____

_____

Do the benefits seem worth it to you?

_____

_____

_____

_____

_____

_____

Given what you've learned from looking at this, how, specifically, are you going to act and think differently?

_____

_____

_____

_____

_____

_____

_____

EXTRA REASSURANCE

But wait!, you say. *She's* still the reason I'm so unhappy—it's what *she's* doing, not me! If I didn't have her in my life, I'd be just fine. The only reason I'm stressed and miserable and can't stand her is because of *her* actions, not mine. Why make *me* do all the work here? Why should I have to suffer *even more,* doing all this self-analysis and self-improvement while she's doing such lousy crap already and getting away with it?

Why? Well, put it this way . . . .

If you were stuck in a prison in a foreign country for ten years and no one knew where you were and there was no chance of getting out until much, much later, but you had a little window and a tiny cot and the chance to move around inside your little cell and were relatively unscathed, all things considered . . . you'd *find* a way to create happiness. You'd have no other choice but to work on your thoughts and emotions, and you'd do your best to craft some sense of purpose and meaning and order for your days.

Lucky for you, you only have to deal with a pesky (or granted, perhaps worse at times) ex-wife or stepmother, not a 6x6 prison cell with a dirt floor. So make the best of it and work with what you have, which is mainly *you* in this situation.

As Buddha once said, "Let us rise up and be thankful, for if we didn't learn a lot today, at least we learned a little, and if we didn't learn a little, at least we didn't get sick, and if we got sick, at least we didn't die; so, let us be thankful."

We never met the guy, but we bet Buddha would have loved crayons. Maybe you do too. That's why this chapter goes out with a bang!

MY VERY OWN CRAPTACULAR COLORABLE PIE CHART

This is all for you, just you! For each slice of the pie, color where you are in intensity with this particular shadow aspect. The closer you are to the inside of the pie, the less that this aspect is a problem for you.

If it makes you feel too exposed, then duplicate this circle on a separate piece of paper and either hide it, burn it, or throw it away. As long as you do the exercise in earnest, this information will be stored in your brain somewhere, and the next time you bump up against one of these feelings in real life, you'll know it.

RESOURCES TO EXPLORE

Books
- *The Power of Now: A Guide to Spiritual Enlightenment,* by Eckhart Tolle
- *Thank You for Being Such a Pain: Spiritual Guidance for Dealing with Difficult People,* by Mark Rosen
- *Quiet Your Mind,* by John Selby

Web sites
- Interlude Retreat (www.interluderetreat.com)
- 32 Keys (www.32keys.com)
- Steve Pavlina's Personal Development for Smart People (www.stevepavlina.com)

AS WE LEAVE THE CHAPTER

Phew! You're done with one of the most difficult chapters in the book! Way to go!

If reading this section was like shoveling horse poop from a swimming pool then hosing it down afterward (isn't everything?), then you're primed and ready for the next section, which involves unicorns and rainbows.

Not really.

But we will be moving onward and upward into dreams, fantasies, and pleasant, reverie-like what-ifs. It's darkest before the dawn. If you're ready for some lightness for a change, then read on.

3
Imagine the Benefits
(Dreams Pull You Forward)

LIGHTER BUT STRONGER!

*In the last chapter, we focused on the complicated mixture of unpleasant thoughts and feelings that keep you stuck in an adversarial position with the other woman. If we removed all of that negativity, would all of your problems with the other woman be solved? Sure, your life would be better without a bunch of ankle-deep garbage. But that's not enough! Here, we're going to talk about how your life might work if there were an actual **partnership** between you two, if you operated more from a place of collaboration.*

*Don't worry. We're not asking you to make that leap yet in this chapter. We're just asking you to **consider the possibility**. Doing so will help you create your own renewable fuel to power through any hard times up ahead.*

*But first, a few memories from us, fittingly, **together.***

A LOOK BACK FROM US

Holding our breath

In the beginning, there didn't seem to be any reason to try to make things any better with each other. If we could just minimize contact with each other for . . . oh . . . the next twelve years or so, we'd be just fine.

But it became harder and harder to "minimize contact" as Carol and David actually got married and all of our lives intertwined. There were school events, family events, and holidays to negotiate.

So what finally changed? Why did anything change?

Well, we got tired of all the animosity.

Simple as that.

Okay, so that was the *beginning* of things changing between us, but it started there.

In some comical, frozen-arms-forward, blindfolded manner, we each took a few lurching stumbles toward the other in the hopes of thawing our relationship and creating at least a more well-oiled "business machine." We were the two hands-on parents and we were stuck with consistent, regular contact, for better or worse.

Wobbly babies

There was a period of about a year to a year and a half when we both started taking baby steps toward each other. Oddly, David (Carol's husband, Jennifer's ex) was the channel through which we both sometimes broadcast our good intentions. He also ended up in the middle of a few misunderstandings, when one or both of us had our feelings hurt through some perceived slight, playing the peacemaker. That must have been strange, and at times, we know it was really tricky.

On more than one occasion, we would each vent to him about the other woman. He would confide a personal detail about the other person in an attempt to help. Sometimes those personal details ended up being the source of additional arguments between the two of us. It always felt like we had to watch out for landmines.

It wasn't easy to keep shooting for harmony. Sometimes, we'd both feel really exposed and vulnerable, and odd too, wondering why we were bothering. People would ask us why we were letting the other person "get away with things," as if they were uncomfortable with our getting along, anticipating the drama.

We'd get somewhere, and then we'd both freeze up for a while, withdrawing from the other.

We both definitely felt like we were in uncharted territory.

One thing that really helped was knowing that the other person was trying *too*. It made us both bite our tongues a bit more. We couldn't so easily badmouth the other person if we were going to be interacting with her again soon. Plus, there was less to feel guilty about if you hadn't just said something nasty about her!

Did it take?

There wasn't any one special memory for either one of us when we both realized "We're friends!", but somehow—eventually—we were. *We had done it.* And we both realized how rare and fragile that friendship was, initially, and took pains to protect it.

Over time, as women do, we tentatively confided in each other and tried to prove to each other that the other's trust wasn't misplaced. We turned to each other for help with parenting problems and, then, with problems in general. Closeness grew. And when we hit rough spots in the road, we did our best to talk about them directly instead of venting elsewhere. Now we don't think there's anything we couldn't talk through.

And neither of us has that sense of the other one trying to undermine us, like we used to. We're working together as a team. We talk about common goals and admit shortcomings where appropriate. Neither one of us has a long, secret list of grievances we're regularly adding to in spidery handwriting anymore. We're no longer invested in trying to prove the other woman is really and truly a bitch.

But we know we're lucky. And we're grateful.

JOURNAL

Have you ever wondered if you and the mother or stepmother could ever get along better than you currently do?

_____

What are your thoughts on this possibility?

_____
_____
_____
_____
_____
_____
_____
_____

If you knew that a better relationship was within your reach with some effort, would you be willing to try? What stands in your way?

_____

_____

_____

_____

_____

_____

_____

_____

A VITAL FUEL

You wouldn't start out on a long road trip without a map, would you? Then visualize, in detail, how good a better relationship could be and use it as your map. It will actually help you *get there,* just like preparing for all the different parts of your journey before you leave. When you finally sit down in the driver's seat, you're so much more likely to feel ready, like "Okay! Let's go! I know where I'm heading . . . ."

This chapter will help you create your own energy source so you can make it over the long haul. That's what makes this one of the most important parts of the book. We're not interested in creating castles in the air that will ultimately depress you. We want to help you create a boost for your journey when you run into tough times.

And as much as we'd love to tell you there won't *be* any more tough times after this section, well, we can't. You already know how difficult these situations can be anyway, especially after slogging through the last chapter! Let's focus on the future, and a few carrots.

WHAT'S IN IT FOR ME?

Who benefits when you reach out to the other woman and start taking steps to reduce the traditional animosity between you two? The short answer? *Everyone.* You're not the only one who suffers when it's stressful between you two. Your problems ripple out into both families. If you were able to calm the nature of your interactions and make them more positive, you'd create a whole *bucketful* of benefits for everyone involved.

The children

Think of what it would be like for the children if you got along with the other woman: less guilt if they like one person or the other better; no more editing their daily life stories; less of a separation between their two lives, internally and externally. They would have a stronger sense of a united family unit, even if it's slow in the making. They could relax, knowing the adults had formed a more cohesive family container that's "holding" them, looking out for them, and taking care.

Put yourself in the children's or stepchildren's shoes for a second. Children are sensitive and empathetic. They can pick up on what adults are *really* feeling, even if the grown-up is trying to pretend otherwise. It must be scary to know that there is such animosity between the two women, a sense of impending doom in the air.

Aside from that, how do you think *you* would do constantly traveling back and forth between families? No sooner do you leave one house, then *ptooey*, you're spit out from a cannon into the other. You come back home, and it's the same thing, *schpack!* Wouldn't you feel grumpy and out of sorts? You can't remove the transitions, but you can make them a *lot* more seamless for the kids.

A box of goodies

Here's what you stand to gain if you work on creating a bridge between yourself and the other woman:

- Another hands-on parent who knows the ins and outs of the kids' issues.
- Better communication, such as fewer flubbed-up meetings, school details, and forgotten belongings traveling between the two houses.
- Someone to call who potentially has a fresh, new perspective when you're stumped by parenting issues.

- Someone to share good news with.
- Someone to befriend who knows your world intimately like few others, even close friends.

And the main benefit for you? Less stress, less stress, less stress. *Whew.* Don't you feel better already?

All the grown-ups

If this one link is strong and reliable, your family and hers are much more likely to be stable and able to weather the inevitable gale-force winds that blow into our lives. All families have to deal with the potential realities of teenage insanity: drugs and alcohol, sex, driving, and emotional issues. You may as well deal with them together and do a better job of it.

The romantic partnerships

And then there's your romantic partnership. If you're the stepmom, obviously, you're in one. There's less animosity that you're channeling every day, fewer vent sessions that have to be listened to. Less time wasted grumbling. There's more room for lightness and happiness. If you're the ex-wife, you may or may not have a partner. Either way, there's just less complaining for everyone involved.

TWO PARALLEL REALITIES FOR MAXINE AND STEPHANIE

Two houses on the same street

Consider two parallel realities for Stephanie, the average stepmother, and Maxine, the ex-wife we met in the first chapter. Same households. Same people. Two totally different experiences and outcomes.

Stomach-knotting world #1

Maxine is running around, yelling at the kids to get their things ready, taking her anger at Stephanie out on her kids. She's stressed because the house is a wreck after homework and school projects, too much to do at work, and a few lousy nights of sleep for everyone this week. She normally makes sure at least the living room looks presentable, quickly shoving items without homes into the laundry room and her bathroom if need be, but she just hasn't had the time.

The kids are stressed because Mom is freaking out. They know she doesn't like Stephanie, even though they *kind of* do. Sometimes they feel bad about this, like they're cheating on their mom. They wish their dad was picking them up instead, but he's been really busy lately, so they're dragging their feet. Why does their mother always run around picking up before Stephanie comes over anyway? Stephanie doesn't care what the house looks like. Sometimes it's messy at Dad's house, too.

Stephanie is in her car, cursing at the traffic, which is unusual for her. She snarls at a driver who cuts her off. She flips the stations, unsuccessfully trying to find a song to bump her into a better mood. All she knows is, the kids *had better* be ready. The last thing she wants to do is stand in Maxine's doorway or, heaven forbid, the living room, and wait in *her* house. She pulls up in front of the driveway, and her heart sinks. How she hates coming here.

New and improved world #2

The kids are dragging their feet again, as they always do whenever they need to get anywhere on time. Their mom tries to stay on them so they won't be late and make Stephanie wait. The house is a wreck after a particularly rough week, but Maxine's not going to feel bad about it. Even though *their* house is usually cleaner, she's not going to engage in "contest-thinking." So they live in a pigsty here sometimes, so be it. It hasn't killed anyone . . . *yet*.

Maxine stands in the doorway of her youngest child Courtney's room, making sure she's packed her clothes. She gives everyone a general reminder of the time and tries to help the kids remember what to take, especially things she knows are important to them, like a favorite toy, tech-gizmo, stuffed animal to sleep with, or new clothes. She's looking forward to a few moments of peace after everyone leaves.

Stephanie finishes the end of one of her favorite songs on the radio, not because she's trying to prolong her isolation, just because she's enjoying herself. She thinks about surprising the kids with a stop at Clogged Artery Burger on the way home and wonders what Maxine's been up to.

Stomach-knotting world #1

The doorbell rings, and all hell breaks loose as the dogs rush to defend their fortress from a known threat at the door (judging from their master's behavior). Maxine struggles to drag Fang and Fido to the backyard, cursing Stephanie again under her breath for making her life miserable. She inwardly curses her ex-husband, too. She looks around at all the papers, art supplies, dirty socks, and backpacks and various toys scattered on the floor, and her chest tightens. Maxine yells in an angry voice for Courtney and Michael to come before she opens the door. Shame at her own feelings of hatred and helpless anger flood her body.

On the other side of the door, Stephanie is longing for a trapdoor (for herself? for Maxine?) and technological advances that would make the teleportation of children instantly possible. She smiles wickedly as she makes a mental connection between the aggressive nature of the dogs and their owner. She idly ponders the many benefits of divorce.

New and improved world #2

The doorbell rings and the dogs go insane, as usual. Maxine drags them outside while announcing what the kids already know, it's time to go. While the children's things aren't near the door as they're supposed to be, she knows that they're packed up and ready, for the most part. Now it's just a matter of rounding up the savages, which can sometimes feel like sand slipping through her fingers. She takes a deep breath before she opens the door and makes a conscious effort to calm herself, wanting to be able to connect with Stephanie from a warmer, more peaceful place. Stephanie looks around at the plants outside the door and wishes she had more time to learn about gardening. What was that she needed to pick up at the store? And there's a school conference coming up that they need to follow up on soon. She's happy to see Maxine, even though she can see Maxine's a bit stressed. She's glad she'll be giving her a break for a few days.

Stomach-knotting world #1

Maxine opens the door and looks in the general direction of Stephanie's face but does not make eye contact with her. "Hang on, I'll get them," she mumbles in a tight voice. She is aware of the fact that Stephanie looks well-put together, whereas she is not wearing any makeup. A quick glance at her harried appearance in the mirror makes her heart sink and then grow instantly hard. Meanwhile, outside the door, Stephanie's heart rate has practically doubled and her blood pressure has climbed to an unhealthy level. It will take a good thirty minutes for it to go back down to normal after they leave. She listens to the chaos unfolding inside the house. She has not been asked inside, nor would she want to go in. But she did catch a glimpse of the living room. *Doesn't this woman ever clean? No wonder they're divorced!*

New and improved world #2

Maxine opens the door and greets Stephanie with a somewhat frazzled smile. "Hey, how's it going? Come on in. They're ready, but I need to round them up. How was traffic?" They make a moment's small talk until Maxine interrupts and asks Stephanie to hang on before she belts out a summons that could possibly be heard across the world. They make a bit more small talk, catching up on a few details about the kids or current events or whatever, until Maxine interrupts again. She asks Stephanie to have a seat while she goes off to grab the children by the extra skin of their necks and carry them back, one by one, like a mother cat. Stephanie chuckles and shakes her head at the madness of it all, but with affection. She knows what this feels like, this herding of cats.

Stomach-knotting world #1

The children are standing by the open door, somewhat sullen, aware of the stress between the two women. They feel awkward and caught in the middle—like they're *supposed* to show their mother that they prefer her, but they're also guilty over loving their mother so much despite all the efforts Stephanie *does* make, even if sometimes they can't stand her. Sometimes they're happy to get away from their mom too. They don't know what to think.

Stephanie notices with some alarm that she is not breathing! If she could just get outside—*now*. She calculates the seconds until her freedom. Maxine gives each child a hug and kiss and pinches up her face as she imagines the neglect that awaits them in the immediate future (such as bedtime or mealtime . . . or anything in between). She only says goodbye to the children, not Stephanie. Stephanie mentally grumbles an insult involving profanity as the door is closed.

New and improved world #2

The children are standing close to the front door with Maxine and Stephanie. Maxine explains that Michael might be coming down with something, unless there's homework he's actually trying to get out of. Stephanie says she knows *just* the magic combination of orange juice and a fizzy vitamin drink that might do the trick. Courtney whines that she wants some too, and both women roll their eyes and exchange a knowing smile. Maxine hugs and kisses the kids, says bye to all, and closes the door with relief.

Stephanie feels a happy sense of chaos as they all pile into the car. She never would have thought things could have worked out this well, but as she checks her charges in the backseat through her rearview mirror, she smiles to herself. This wasn't what she had imagined for a family when she was younger, but she'll take it. There's love and tenderness here, support from many different directions, and an enduring steadiness that makes her feel like everything will be okay, despite the daily chaos of life with children.

This is the perfect opportunity to focus a little more closely on the kids, now that you've got some visuals in your head.

Keeping the focus on you and your problems, instead of what's best for the kids

Stepmoms and moms can be such convenient targets, especially if you're holding a grudge, competing against each other, or getting all stressed about money issues. But all that emotional turmoil comes at a cost, and it's usually the youngest members of the family who pay. If you find yourself falling into these behaviors too often, it's time to snap out of it:

- You're often annoyed by things your kids or stepkids are trying to tell you and are only semi-listening.
- You wish they would just leave you alone most of the time so you can stew in your own thoughts about the other woman.
- You're churlish and snappy when going on about regular household chores, leaking your irritation and emotional angst all over everyone.

We can all periodically get caught up in an inner storm of self-absorption, but just letting yourself coast along for too long is not okay!

For moms: What's your current state of connection with your kids? Is there anything going on with the stepmom that you need to step back from and put away in a mental drawer for a bit?

_____
_____
_____
_____
_____
_____
_____

For stepmoms: What's your current state of connection with your step-children? Is there anything you need to step back from that's going on between your husband and ex-wife for a bit?

_____
_____
_____
_____
_____

_____

_____

_____

OVERVIEW OF THE SPECIFIC BENEFITS

All right, all right, we've convinced you. It's better to get along with each other; anyone could figure that out. But here's what you need to keep in mind when you start doubting whether making the effort is worth it:

I do, for the last time

We're going to talk about this first, because the marriage or romantic partnership is one of the primary structures of nurturing for the children, on both sides. It needs to be strong so that children don't have to go through another divorce. There is a higher rate of divorce for remarried families (up to 75 percent when children are involved, as opposed to 60 percent without children), so they are even more at risk.

Did you know there are now more recombined families than nuclear families because of the accumulation of divorced and stepfamilies? Sad, but true. We have to learn to work *with* the new dual-family landscape, instead of against it, because it's here to stay.

When the two women get along, it removes a lot of the animosity between the households. The husband and stepmother have a lot less to gossip about, and so do the mother and her partner. Without the nasty backbiting, there will be fewer misunderstandings and less of a sense of competition between the two women, and the two households. The man will feel less caught in the middle.

All of a sudden, instead of feeling like there is someone out to actively undermine the marriages or romantic partnerships, that enemy is gone. Now it's just back to the regular couple against the world, like normal people. Now the focus can be on work, money, friendships, creating a happy, healthy union, and especially, on being a good parent.

We all have the tendency to dissect the behavior of those we know well. But when things start to actually work between a stepmother and a mother, a mechanism seems to kick in that's a part of the way women do friendships. They begin to feel protective of their new friend, less likely to want to eviscerate her, even if that's what they were used to doing before. They feel more inclined to bite their tongue and cut her some slack.

Wow, I think I can breathe again

How can we possibly say enough about this? Having a harmonious relationship with the other woman is the closest you can come to having a magic wand that erases a substantial portion of angst from your life. Instead of resorting to a habitual pattern of focusing on what she did wrong today, this week, or last month, you're suddenly free to just—*not*. You'll be happier and more relaxed. Think how much better you'll feel if you're not carrying around so much resentment, frustration, and anger.

You won't have to worry so much about all the things you're saying about her anymore. You won't have to worry about covering up your gossip, or hiding your real feelings from the kids, or keeping track of any lies or ways that you might have fudged the truth.

You're freer for all the best reasons.

Less flour in your hair

Who couldn't use help with parenting? It's overwhelming at times, confusing at others, and the requirements are constantly changing. What was appropriate for a three-year-old is hopelessly inadequate for a five-year-old. What works for a tween is insulting to a teenager. And then there are all the different personalities if you have more than one child.

The more support you can get adjusting to the changing needs and challenges of parenting, the better for your sanity, and the better it is for the child.

Households can now focus on creating organization and success, instead of shooting the other side down through passive-aggressive, competitive behavior. Instead of expending energy on blame and fault-finding, both sides can now try to help things work as smoothly as possible.

There are a million logistical things to handle with children: school and homework, friends and playdates, developmental changes, behaviors and consequences, health issues, birthdays, holidays, presents, etc. May as well use your resources to tackle *that!*

If you're the mom, remember what it was like when the dad came home and you could jump right into talking about something that had to do with the kids? There was no need for explanations about what one child was like or the other, it was already understood. If you're the stepmother, you have that with your husband.

Well, it's possible to have that same sense of a "shorthand" with all the adults, to be able to communicate with someone else who's up on the latest developments and various solutions that you're trying to implement.

There's an incredible sense of relief and comfort in knowing you have support in your efforts to be a good parent. If you're the mom and you didn't have this kind of support in your marriage, this may be a new experience for you. It's also possible that your improved situation with the stepmom might even make parenting easier between you and your ex.

Imagine being able to breathe easy, knowing the other person is not going to try to prove you wrong, jump on your faults, or act superior to you. It's a wonderful feeling of teamwork and partnership. There's a comrade to help pull the cart, carry the load, and shoulder the burden.

A house *not* made of straw

When you work together, the kids do not constantly have to figure out two different sets of rules. They don't get to play the two households against each other, or one parent off another. The less conflict there is between the adults between the two houses, the less conflict between siblings.

They don't have to feel as if their lives are split and chaotic. They get to be more integrated people too, instead of two different versions—the kind of people they are at one house and the kind of people they are at the other house. It feels more like one big family unit for the children, however imperfect that unit might be.

The children may not like having a united front. We know our kids have complained bitterly about this. But it's made our lives much easier, and we know we're better parents because of it.

Not only that, once you align some of the rules between houses, your position as an authority is much stronger. We finally got to the point where we helped each other enforce consequences and punishments, which was fairly effective in modifying negative behavior.

It wasn't always easy because sometimes one parent would feel really uncomfortable being "the heavy." Nevertheless, we tried to keep the emphasis on the fact that the rules had been broken and the children had to live with the consequences of their actions.

Also, there were times when we disagreed on the actual consequence but still chose to enforce it to support the other parents. We imposed restrictions for computer and TV time and took away fun options, such as going to a movie, or reduced allowances. The message got through loud and clear with the kids: Break the rules and you can't escape *by going to the other house.* They hated it. We loved it.

Multiplying the brainpower

It's really hard to tackle tough parenting problems all on your own. You second-guess yourself. Your children probably know *exactly* how to push your buttons and manipulate you, or how to play their cards to get their way. But when it's you and at least two other adults, you're much more likely to get a balanced view of the situation, or at least a multifaceted view. After bouncing your ideas around, it's such a relief to sit back, mull over everyone's input, and come up with what feels like a more nuanced, effective response to a tough situation.

Now, instead of it just being you as a stepmother on your own trying to figure this out, or you as a mom without the father as a partner, you have an additional cohort to help you problem-solve tricky behavioral issues. You two might have very different approaches, but you can still learn from each other. Experiment with new ideas and techniques.

Parents can pay more attention to what's actually going on with their kids and attend to problems when they arise, instead of being so absorbed with their own problems and drama. There's also the chance to resolve problems from beginning to end, with a resolution—and chances to make course corrections, instead of having efforts end with the roadblocks that the two households normally put up against each other.

You're listening too, now?

With the adults on the same page, the children are more likely to receive consistent levels of love, nurturing, and support. Instead of not knowing what's going on with one of their children or stepchildren, now the adults are watching and are up on things together. Before, each adult might have had blind spots when it came to each child. Now they have the benefit of the perspective of the other adults. You're much more likely to catch problems before they turn into something really big, or if you're already dealing with something scary that's unraveling, at least there's potential safety from every direction of the net. Your children will feel the difference.

WHAT ABOUT THE MAN?

Even if the ex-husband isn't supportive of the two women improving their relationship, it can still work between the two women. And it's more likely that their doing so will eventually help him come around, once he sees that his worst fears fail to materialize. We've covered some of his concerns in previous chapters. Below are a few more.

He may fear losing the sense of control that he and his "side" already have

The whole idea may just seem too strange and unusual, cross some unhealthy boundaries, or just not seem right somehow. *These two women, getting along, having a connection to each other?* Isn't this at odds with the direction he's trying to go in his life? The ex-wife represents his past and his wife is his present and his future. Isn't mixing those two things up just asking for trouble?

That's the last thing he needs. He's already seen what divorce is like, how painful it is for all involved (no matter who initiated it), how difficult it is to date as a single father and pair up to the point of marriage. Now he's going to risk everything he's gained up until this point to "let" these two women create more of a team?

Also, there just aren't that many good examples out there. If only there were more celebrities doing this (besides Ashton, Demi, and Bruce, and Jada and Will and his ex), it might seem more *normal*. If only talking about this to people at work, or friends or family, didn't elicit such a puzzled, confused, sometimes even wary response. It just seems *weird*.

Whatever his response, each woman will have to come to a decision on her own about what she wants to create in this situation. Remember, even small good experiences may bring him around to eventually supporting the idea.

Since the state of the ex-husband/ex-wife relationship is so important, we'd like to focus on that specifically for a moment. But don't go away, stepmoms, because your input is vital here too. Moms, if you're willing to look at two potentially difficult questions, you might create some wonderful possibilities between you and your ex.

Not seeing him for who he is NOW

Part and parcel of fueling conflict between you and another person is keeping the other person frozen in a story, an unchanging character who's only capable of doing this, this, and this and no more, without chances for improvement or room to grow. Haven't your friends, coworkers, or family ever surprised you? We're all changing, all of the time! Moms, you might think because you once lived with your ex-and knew him well, the mental image still holds. That may be basically true in terms of values and personality, but even then, people are often capable of sweeping transformations.

This can tie back into grieving too if he's re-partnered (more about this in Chapter Four), has other children, etc.—perhaps if you let go of who you think you knew, it might mean you are truly getting left in the dust, as far as what you meant to him, the significance of your past together, etc. See if you can step back and look at your ex from a neutral vantage point. Maybe even a bit of curiosity will arise.

For moms: Who is this person now? In what ways do you need to update your version of who you think he is?

_____

_____

_____

_____

_____

_____

_____

For stepmoms: Are there any ways in which you're keeping your husband stuck in the past? Do you need to update your version of who he is and what he's capable of?

_____

_____

_____

_____

_____

_____

_____

Letting lost opportunities pass you by

Moms, even if you sometimes feel pissy toward your ex, find yourself occasionally shrieking "Argh!" after you get off the phone with him, or wish you could shake him by the shoulders, you might still be able to be friends. Yes. We said friends. 'Course, it takes two people to do this and he may not be willing. But there's nothing to keep you from making little exploratory steps, from extending a few peace offerings here and there.

Jennifer: Believe it or not, David (my ex) is one of the first people I turn to sometimes when I need a kind, listening ear. He knows me inside and out, he's seen the worst sides of me and still actually seems to like me! I get his weird sense of humor, which no one else does, so I'm obligated to continue being his friend out of pity. (See, now he would get that, but it's a fine line, isn't it?) Something we were able to do over the years that got us here was apologize. This seemed to happen in stages, over many conversations, but there no longer seems to be anything we hold against each other from the past. The slate feels clean between us, but we had to work at it, and we both took risks to get here. I'm so glad that the kids don't have to see us fighting anymore, because at first even a divorce didn't prevent that.

Sure, there are tons of benefits to be had by befriending the step-mom in this scenario too, but think of how much better your life might be if the other person who was responsible for bringing your children into the world was also your buddy? Think it's impossible? Never to be? Too weird and harem-like? Think again. What else are you going to do with your life, if not dump all that old baggage?

For moms: What are some of the things you still like and love about your ex-husband? In what ways could you serve as a friend to him? How might this benefit the children in your life?

_____

_____

_____

_____

_____

_____

_____

_____

For stepmoms: How would you feel about your husband and his ex-wife becoming friends? Is there anything you feel like you'd have to give up if this occurred? If this is difficult to imagine, would you be willing to try for the benefit of the children?

_____

_____

_____

_____

_____

_____

_____

Which brings us right up to the front door of our next section.

CREATING A NEW KIND OF FAMILY STRUCTURE

From two separate worlds to one extended family

Once you pave the way with a partnership between the two women, you open the doors for a completely new kind of family.

We don't know exactly what to call it. It's not the same thing as a *blended* family, the term people sometimes use to describe a stepfamily. And we've heard the term *bonus* family, which doesn't quite fit for us, since that sounds like an extra family you won in the mail, or a room you're adding at the back of house. *Second* family sounds confusing, because who gets to be the first?

All we know is, this is a whole new kind of safety net for the children. It's freer of conflict; it could potentially feel warmer, quieter, and happier. If it takes a village to raise more self-sufficient, well-adjusted children, then this is like creating your own little mini-village.

The beauty of it is, you'll be responding to this crisis of two "split" families in the best possible way and creating an entirely new way to live in the process. You'll be pioneers, ahead of the times. You'll be helping to change and strengthen our culture for the better. You'll be at the forefront of a new movement.

Best of all, *and most important,* you'll be doing something powerful to help heal the damage of divorce in each family. When you go through the effort involved to create this new kind of family, you benefit first, but then everyone else will, too.

Find the motivation for *yourself* initially if you must, but know that you'll be taking a revolutionary step, compared to the stereotypical divorced family or stepfamily.

JOURNAL
Would it be nice to be different? Would you feel proud of yourself? Would you be happy for yourself and your partner and the kids and all the other adults involved? Are you starting to get a glimpse of what's possible?

_____

_____

_____

_____

_____

_____

_____

If you're still feeling resistant or hopeless about the whole idea, we'll take a break here and do some doodling to lighten things up.

Quiz: Fears you may have about getting along

See if you can relate to the worries below. Get out some colored pencils or colored markers or just use a pen or pencil, if that's all you have. For each statement, fill in the bar to rate the level of intensity, as shown in the sample scale.

Here's a sample scale:

| Less intense | In the middle | Almost unbearable |

Now I'll have to be nice all the time.

Now I'll have to forgive her for all the unfair things she's already done.

[ ]

If we get along, then I can't show her how much she's hurt me. I have to bury all that.

[ ]

I'll have to be more flexible and yielding than I'm comfortable with.

[ ]

I can't do things my way anymore.

[ ]

It's just too weird and uncomfortable; I don't want to.

[ ]

I'll feel too exposed.

[ ]

I know she's only going to use this to pounce on me later, when I least expect it.

[ ]

This is impossible, only rare, "evolved" people can do this; I don't have what it takes and neither does she.

[ ]

I won't be able to just be myself anymore; what if I really need to stick to my guns sometimes?

[ ]

I'll end up giving her too much power and the kids will suffer for it.

[ ]

Everyone will think I'm a pansy for ceding control.

[ ]

Isn't doing it this way just *wrong* somehow?

[ ]

What did you discover about your greatest fears and resistance? Now that you know these things about yourself, you'll be more apt to catch yourself the next time these thoughts and feelings arise. Pay attention when you see this dynamic playing itself out in your life and see if you can make some different choices. More about this in Chapter Four.

STEPPING BACK AND ASSESSING

A few questions as we wrap up.

Will you answer the call to create something new? Do you see the advantages to at least *trying* for this? Are you willing to be brave and venture into new and untested waters?

What's being modeled for the children in your life when it comes to conflict resolution and human relationships?

_____

_____

_____

_____

_____

_____

_____

_____

_____

EXTRA REASSURANCE

What if your dreams seem hopeless? What if where you are and where you want to be seem so far away from one another that the thought of attempting this makes you as limp as a heatstroke victim? What if you feel overwhelmed and defeated before you've even begun?

Take it one moment at a time, one breath at a time. You can't fix relationships overnight. Start out small and set your sights higher when you have a few successes under your belt. Jump ahead to Chapter Eight if you need more immediate help to calm your fears and your feelings.

Me, myself, and I

It's possible that you may find you're the only person trying to make things better between the two of you. This happens. Rather than just emphasizing how good it feels to bask in the glow of moral superiority, we'll gently turn you in the direction of, again, your own personal sense of peace.

Even if your worst fears come true and the other woman continues to be as strong and impenetrable as a medieval wall, this book still applies to you. You'll learn more about the other woman's world, which can help create understanding, compassion, and, eventually, a simple serenity, even if it's just you, sitting under the tree by yourself.

By carefully considering this subject of mother/stepmother relationships, you're planting seeds in your brain that will quietly and subtly influence your own feelings and behavior. A part of you will now be paying closer attention to the ways in which you undermine, or support, harmony between the two of you.

Quiz: Where do you feel hopeful?

Here's a chance to imagine where you might be able to make progress if you and the other woman got along better. What are your dreams? What are you shooting for?

Gauge your present *feeling of hope* for each category. Color in the pie chart by starting in the middle for each slice and shading outward. The closer to the outside you are, the more positive you feel about this possibility.

Stronger marriages and romantic partnership

Less personal stress; more peace

More brainpower for problem-solving

Better parenting

Less competition between the two households

Stability and consistency for the kids

Sympathy from a fellow "insider"

RESOURCES TO EXPLORE

Books
- *The 7 Habits of Highly Effective Families,* by Stephen R. Covey
- *Connections: The Threads that Strengthen Families,* by Jean Illsey Clarke
- *Giving the Love That Heals: A Guide for Parents,* by Harville Hendrix

Web sites
- Pathway to Happiness (www.pathwaytohappiness.com/happiness)
- Brain, Child (www.brainchildmag.com)
- Literary Mama (www.literarymama.com)

AS WE LEAVE THE CHAPTER

You've heard enough about *why* to do this. And if you followed the exercises in earnest in Chapter Two, you've made some room inside yourself for change to happen. In the next chapter, we're going to show you *how* to do this. It's not as complicated as you think, and you can start out by doing something surprisingly simple.

4
Take Action
(Stretching, Inside and Out)

THE DIFFERENCE BETWEEN SITTING AND WALKING

*Thus far, you've gotten a sense of the big picture, looked at ways you're undermining progress, and lastly, imagined some healthy, happy possibilities. Now, we're going to show you **how** to actually go about doing this.*

*We'll start off with some changes you'll be making inside your **head** (internal actions) and then we'll focus on a few experiments you'll undertake in **real life** (external actions).*

But first, we'll talk a bit about how this part of the process went for us.

A LOOK BACK FROM US

Jennifer: It sounds so simple, but honestly, change started with our hellos.

I think the first few times I tried to say, "Hey, how's it going?" like I meant it, Carol just looked at me, surprised. Her astonishment was instantly replaced with suspicion, as in *What is she trying to get from me?* And probably most important, *How can I get her out of my face?*

I tried to use my much-improved relationship with David (my ex, Carol's husband) to convey that I wanted to change things with Carol. (I'd already worked on forgiving him and making amends.) Once Carol got the message that I was extending a teeny, little olive branch, however wilted and leafless it was, she eventually stuck out her branch through a crack in the door, too.

There's nothing like seeing that someone is trying to make you try more.

But I have to admit, I was scared taking those first steps. I didn't want her to think I was after David or trying to interfere with their lives. I was well aware of the fact that most ex-wives have no place in their ex-husbands' new families, and that's simply that. I was also afraid that she would see my efforts as an admission of guilt somehow, or admitting I was wrong. I was nervous about her possibly using my vulnerabilities to gain the upper hand and then humiliating me.

But she was never aggressive with me. When she was upset about something, she would simply avoid me. I could tell a lot by whether she lifted her head to greet me from the kitchen or not. Head down: bad. Head up and saying hello: hopeful possibilities.

The very first time we ever did something alone, just the two of us, was when we went out to dinner to discuss the possibilities of writing this book. It was weird, sitting in the restaurant together, eating pizza. Part of me kept thinking, *look who I'm sitting with! This is bizarre!*

Once we had a few successes behind us, we felt even more inspired to extend ourselves. And it became harder to be a jerk to her or David, to be rigid and inflexible, even though there were times I think we all sometimes felt like we were losing ground by being so damned cooperative!

So start with hello and see what happens. It's not like it was the solution for everything for us, but it was the definitely the beginning of something new.

Carol: It would have been so incredibly easy to go on hating Jennifer. I had the whole world rooting for me.

But Jennifer stepped up to the plate and really made an effort. They were always little things, and they didn't necessarily have the effect she was going for, but after a bit of time, she wore me down. A smile here, a genuine hello there, an earnest "How's it going?" How about a hug after a real connection?

On my first or second Mother's Day, Jennifer gave me a very simple, elegant card that said something like "Thank you so much for being a great stepmom to my kids." It really moved me. A card shows that you've gone out of your way; it shows you were thinking about the other person. There's intention behind it, it's pre-meditated. There's also something about a card that allows you to say something truly sappy that you could never bring yourself to say in person. And that's how I took it: It was *real*.

I took her words at face value because there was forethought behind them. Also, they had nothing to do with David; they were meant only for *me*.

I couldn't just ignore this the next time I saw her either—I had to thank her. Just imagining that act alone made me realize something. I kept playing out over and over in my head how I might do this, even visualizing giving her a hug, which was something we'd never done before. I mean, physical contact is huge! And whenever I'd imagine that, I'd feel really good. I'd imagine the relief of it all, instead of what it was normally like, not getting along.

But along with all the positive feelings, there were also still the negative ones, because challenges continued to happen. We would go backward on a regular basis, but it was all those good things peppered in there that *eventually* pulled us forward, because the good things went both ways.

She became my friend. And what better place to have a friend than in the enemy's camp? Except gradually, there was no more enemy.

For a while, there were two of her in my mind. The Jennifer I liked and got along with and the Jennifer I disagreed with about parenting/money/etc. issues. I had to keep them separate so I could move forward with our relationship. Eventually, I realized that you can love someone without having to like everything about her.

Creating a harmonious relationship with the other woman is a very gradual process and it doesn't happen overnight. But it can work.

THINGS TO PONDER BEFORE YOU ACT

An inner shift
It all starts here: You lay down your weapons. *Choose* to make things better between you two. Just decide, whether her behavior changes or not.

Accept that you're the only person you can really control. And take complete and total responsibility for the situation you've created inside your own head and heart. Where else could you possibly start?

Do it for *you* first, then for your marriage or partnership (if you're in one—the mom might be single, dating, or remarried). Then do it for the kids, because you're the adult and you're the one who's supposed to be acting with maturity and consideration for the long haul.

Decide to end the war, just decide. Even if the ex-wife or stepmother in your life is actively doing everything in her power to hurt you, your significant other, or the children, see if you can make a decision from a clear place: your highest, wisest self. Do what's necessary to secure a sense of healthy protection (more about this in a moment), then move on from there.

If you hold back on making this decision first, and then try to move forward with outward changes, it will be like pressing down on a car's accelerator while keeping the brakes on. You'll feel disoriented and conflicted. You'll still be looking for reasons to blame her and make it her fault when it doesn't work.

Now that may sound easy for us to say, because we're writing a *book* together. Nevertheless, *you're* the one inside your own head. You're both the organ grinder and the monkey, chattering away upstairs; defining, characterizing, categorizing. You decide whether things are good or bad, hopeful or hopeless.

So it's up to you.

Will you take this on? Genuinely?

Good. Now let's create a foundation for success and help your subconscious mind know that there's someone looking out for you. And that would be *you*.

Determine your walls

How do you create a balance between the openness necessary for change and protection for when you feel threatened? By using boundaries or walls—we all have them. Some folks are tough nuts to crack. Others may as well have boundaries made of Swiss cheese. But definitely, they're a good and necessary device for maintaining sanity and peace.

Being stuck with an ex-wife or stepmom in your life is akin to having an uncomfortably close relationship with a relative you're not sure you even *like*. There are ways that you do *not* want her involved in your life, some areas that are off-limits. For example, you'd prefer to keep your romantic life or marriage, health issues, and certain types of family situations private.

Think of boundaries in terms of two *types*.

One wall or boundary is strong and impermeable because it protects you from hostile, unhealthy elements, such as acts of reckless irresponsibility and outright deceit. With this type of wall, you create a moat around you and do whatever you can to minimize the chances of a breach. (If you're dealing with some of the really big issues, like substance abuse or suspected child abuse, please seek out professional help.)

The other wall is more permeable and that's okay. It's also meant to protect you, but it can be lowered at will if the other person has been deemed safe enough. Consider the other person in this partnership. Where are you willing to open up around the other woman? Where can you drop your defenses? Is it possible to refrain from striking back if you feel offended? Where can you give a little? Or even *forgive?*

You let people know where your boundaries are by establishing clear limits: *You may treat me this way, but not like this.* Think through a potential scenario where your limits might be tested. Imagine how you would convey your boundaries to the other person. Would you state your preferences? Walk away? Disengage? You have the right to establish the perimeters of acceptable interactions for you.

Healthy walls are vital, and you should know what yours are. It might help to figure them out based on values. Go *deep*: What's important to you? What result are you trying to create? What's nonnegotiable? Up for consideration?

If your boundaries are unclear, take a closer look from a place of curiosity. Deciphering your boundaries will help you troubleshoot current problems and pave the way for future progress.

JOURNAL

Think about this issue a few moments and write down your impressions.

Are there any areas of my life that feel like they need a little more protection? What can I do to create this?

_____

_____

_____

_____

_____

_____

_____

_____

What are some of my healthy non-negotiable walls or boundaries?

_____

_____

_____

_____

_____

_____

_____

Are there any walls of mine that seem to be more of a hindrance than a help?

_____

_____

_____

_____

_____

_____

_____

In what ways am I willing to "give a little" with the other woman?

_____

_____

_____

_____

_____

_____

_____

_____

_____

Once you feel clearer about creating a foundation of safety, you're ready for the next step.

Yielding

Maybe at this point, you're willing to admit the other woman might have a few good qualities scattered about, here and there. But what do you do if, whenever you feel yourself softening toward her, it's immediately stopped in its tracks by the memories of incriminating evidence rushing to the fore?

The solution lies in a simple little word that's come to seem so cliché and old-fashioned that we don't ever really seem to *hear* what it means anymore: forgiveness.

Turns out there's a lot of confusion about it. Here's what forgiveness is *not:*

- saying you're okay with what someone has done to you if he or she has harmed you
- approving of everything else the person does
- liking the person and completely accepting him or her
- feeling free of hurt feelings and leftover anger
- automatically wanting to be closer to the other person
- having to love the other person

Here's what forgiveness is:

- a setting aside of the suffering and betrayal you've been carrying around in your heart
- a releasing of the pain and anger and hatred, as best you can
- an offer of a new start, a blank slate, for yourself and the other person
- a demarcation between the past and the present, though you understand the future might be difficult, too

The difference between the two is the *openness,* the letting go. That matters because the suffering and the betrayal live in you. You keep them alive with your broken-record thought/emotion loops to which all humans are susceptible.

Forgiveness often initially happens for *you.* You say to yourself: I will stop the mutual energy drain of attack and defend. I may feel vulnerable, but I also trust myself to take care of myself. I will lay the groundwork for something new to happen. I will make myself blank, neutral, empty.

Can you allow your heart to soften toward the other person and feel compassion for both her and yourself?

Try a little tenderness

Compassion is not the same thing as giving your stamp of approval, either. Compassion is the acknowledgment that we are *all* human. We all occasionally act from a place of self-interest and self-protection, and we often make mistakes, even if this is not how we would *like* for ourselves to behave. Compassion is the expression of a certain kind of sympathy and *tenderness* in the face of our very human frailties.

Can you have compassion for yourself while you do something new and perhaps a little frightening? It can be hard and uncomfortable to change. Can you cultivate a feeling of sympathy and understanding for the other woman, too?

Rather than jumping back to old familiar patterns and making her wrong if she doesn't react the way you'd like her to, see if you can detect her pain and suffering—and not from a place of glee, either! See if you can sense some nervousness, some fear, or anxiety about letting her guard down. If it's nerve-wracking for you, it's probably scary for her, too.

Compassion creates a bridge from you to others. It has nothing to do with one-upmanship or being stronger, smarter, or wiser. See if you can open your heart a little bit and be kind to yourself, then kind toward her.

If you have difficulty making this leap, think of someone you love dearly and hold them in your mind and heart. Tune into the natural feelings of love and warmth that you have for that person. Then imagine the other woman, and see if you can "slide" that feeling over to her. You won't lose anything. It's not going to hurt you. And you might be surprised by how much this can help.

I need to know what's around the corner!

An unpleasant reality about change: You never know what's coming. You might feel unsteady and uncertain, like something is about to whiz around the corner and knock you down. Can you learn how to make friends with uncertainty? Can you get comfortable with being in that space of not knowing?

The next time you find yourself trying to force an issue just so you can gauge how it's likely to play out, stop yourself. Do nothing. Distract yourself. Give the issue some breathing room.

Then, see what happens, all on its own.

Sometimes, the more you get out of your own way, the better. It's a habit that can be cultivated.

What you really, really want

Remember all that uncomfortable work you did in Chapter Two about owning your own crap? If you're scratching your head in confusion because you, uh . . . skipped that part, looking for the light and happy stuff, we're going to kindly ask you to go back and read it again. You can't clean up the mess in the corner if you won't turn the light on to find it!

If you *did* do the work in Chapter Two, then congratulations. You know what we're hinting at in this section already, right? Keep checking in with yourself to see what's motivating your actions. Are you still trying to make her wrong by doing this better?

Not everyone will be receptive to your efforts to improve things. Not everyone will meet your efforts with understanding. For some women, it may indeed be just one more opportunity to gain the upper hand. But often, people respond to genuine warmth with hesitation or confusion at first, and then . . . curiosity, and then . . . a guarded openness. If all goes well, that can turn into a lovely kind of melting between two people.

Just remember, one fuel that keeps a feud going is feeling like the other side hates you. It creates an odd mixture of shame, anger, and embarrassment. Do you hate her because you know she hates you, and you want to hate her back?

If you still find yourself wanting to compete with her, take another look at the results you were hoping to create in Chapter Three. And think about how a sense of competition affects the way you speak.

Bite your tongue

Here's the deal: no more verbal digs, even subtle ones. You don't get to make little snide remarks aloud anymore. You don't get to gossip like crazy about the other woman to "burn off some steam." You don't get to release tension and anger by venting and making her wrong with the intention of feeling better about yourself at the end.

You just need to . . . *not say anything.* Hard to do, but so, so wise.

This may feel like you're making an enormous sacrifice (especially if you know that she's still talking trash about you), but if you do it, you'll gain one huge benefit almost immediately.

No guilt. Which only makes the next step that much easier.

Strengthen your coping skills

What can you do today, right now, to create more peace inside your own mind and spirit? What can you do to calm the waters of your thought processes? No one else is in there besides you—no matter what the other woman is doing.

What can you do to dissolve stress, to relax, to process negativity? What can you do to discharge negative emotions? Can you meditate? Exercise? Journal? Do you have any therapeutic processes you can fall back on to transform difficult feelings and situations?

If nothing else, you can always fall back on the simplest of solutions: take a deep breath. And follow that up with several more. A deep breath calms your nervous system and affects the chemical stew that your brain produces. Periodically notice whether you're breathing deeply, and if not, it's simple enough to fix.

It's in your best interests and the interests of your family to get better at managing stress, to in fact be even *amazing* at this. Make it a goal: get really, really good at reducing nerves and heightened anxiety.

So inhale and get cracking! Explore, learn, research, ask around, and get online. See which self-help books jump out at you. Track down some free or low-cost therapy (if finances are a concern).

For more tools for creating peace and calm on the fly, refer to Chapter Eight.

WHAT ABOUT THE MAN?

A united front

How can you set the stage for success with the husband/ex-husband? Where would you like to go? What stands in your way? We're going to take a moment to really focus on how each woman's relationship with this person might be contributing to the problems she's having.

For starters, how does he feel about the idea of the two women becoming potential friends and "business partners"? Does he feel threatened, imagining a loss of privacy? Does he seem wary and worried?

JOURNAL

For moms: How does your ex-husband seem to feel about the possibility of you and the stepmother getting along? How does this affect how much effort you are willing to put into this situation?

_____

_____

_____

_____

_____

_____

_____

_____

For stepmoms: How does your husband seem to feel about the possibility of you and the mother getting along? How does this affect how much effort you are willing to put into this situation?

_____

_____

_____

_____

_____

_____

Both women: Let him know you will not gossip about him. Let him know that your priority is preserving the marriage and keeping the sanctity of that private and sacred. Let him know that, even if it all sounds kind of unusual and strange, it could actually be a really good thing for you two to get along, *especially for the kids.*

In the spirit of creating a totally cleaned out inner house in preparation for change, we want to take a look at regrets, and this part in particular is addressed to the moms (with questions for the stepmom, too). You may have come a long way already in terms of releasing anger and resentments. If so, bravo! But we do know from experience that regrets can sometimes be lurking in the background of our psyches, unexpressed. When they are, their presence can sometimes make it difficult to move forward.

Refusing to mourn

There's one big reason we're willing to spend so much of our emotional lives stewing in animosity with our ex, and it ain't pretty. Not only does it have to do with ugly-face crying (you know the kind, it's what Academy Award–winning actresses do so well), it's also almost unbearable to experience. We're talking sorrow here; sadness—big, sweeping, aching voids.

> **Jennifer:** *I remember one day in the garage, cleaning out paper grocery bags stuffed to the brim with first squiggles; outlines of traced hands from kindergarten; sweet art projects and first writings. For some reason, I'd been avoiding this task for years and wasn't even sure why. As I sat on the floor, sifting through one drawing of "our family" after another, I finally lost it and starting sobbing—the wracking, snorting kind that makes you feel like you can't breathe. Our little family—tall dad, less tall mom, one bigger child, a toddler—we were no more. At least, not as we were in the pictures.*
>
> *I'd cried about our divorce before, but this was different. No longer was my crying mixed with anger and thoughts of making my ex wrong. It was just overwhelming grief and sadness; the deep, shredding disappointment of a course of action that was immutable and damaging to all of us. Sure, we're human and we've all adapted. But to face the truth and sharpness of my tears so fully was grueling.*

For moms: So what's left in you to mourn? Are you afraid if you let the pain surface, it will have no end? If you fish around inside, do you sense there's a dam that needs unblocking?

_____

_____

_____

_____

_____

_____

_____

_____

_____

_____

For stepmoms: What continues to cause you grief? What needs mourning in your situation with your husband? Is there anything that needs to be released? Are you holding things in like a trooper?

_____

_____

_____

_____

_____

_____

_____

Phew! What a note to end on, huh? We went out with a bang.

So now that we've covered a good look at our *innards* in this early section, it's time we moved on to taking action in the real world.

EXTERNAL ACTIONS

In the first part of this chapter, we asked you to make a decision: to be willing to form a bridge between you and the other woman, no matter where you are now. Initially it might feel like one of those shaky, twisting rope bridges that's going to buck you right off, or—you might get lucky and unite two cliffs with a sturdy log.

This is where you get to put all those ideas into practice and *experiment*. Your efforts might result in success, or they might result in failure. It helps to cultivate the mind-set of a persistent and curious scientist. Are you willing to go through several attempts and subsequent course corrections to create the results you're looking for?

Okay then, *onward!* What does this look like? How do you do it?

WHAT YOU'RE GOING TO ACTUALLY TRY

Let's start at the very beginning.

We recommend starting out with baby steps—bit by bit, day by day, and gesture by gesture. You might begin by simply asking the other woman how she's doing on the phone, or in person, if you'd never normally do that. Offer to loan her a good book you just finished reading or a new CD. Surprise the hell out of her by baking her something (corny as it sounds)—some cookies or banana bread or, hey, make her some home-brewed beer. If you'd like, you could send her an e-mail or a handwritten letter or card (if you can remember how to do this). If you really want to be bold, you could ask her out to coffee. Find something that has to do with the kids that you'd like to share, like a finished project or piece of art.

It doesn't have to be a big awkward experience. Try to choose a gesture that works *for you*—the level of vulnerability; something appropriate to her interests; something that lets you save face if she's not jumping for joy over your magnanimous efforts.

The whole point is to signal a reconciliatory tone on your part, a change in status from adversaries to possible alliances. Wouldn't you start wondering what was happening if she took similar steps with you? It would get you thinking, right?

You're going to try to feel your way into a tiny bit of progress first, *and then* ask for a truce. This isn't the same thing as waving a floppy white flag and surrendering. A truce is a suspension of hostilities *by mutual agreement*. So let's look at how you go about doing that, right after these questions.

JOURNAL

What are some things you'd consider doing to reach out to the stepmom or mom? Can you sense even the tiniest possibility for a happy outcome?

_____

_____

_____

_____

_____

_____

_____

_____

How to ask for (and offer) a truce

It's more than a little scary, thinking of asking someone if she'll lay down her weapons at the exact same time as you do. What's to keep her from quickly picking hers up and gaining the advantage? Nothing! Even though curiosity killed the cat, it might just work here in your favor. We humans are intrigued by anything new and different that we can't figure out.

Whether it's by phone, e-mail, letter or card, or in person, do *something* and get her attention. Then, somehow, some way, in language that feels the most comfortable, tell her:

- You have something to talk to her about. Preface this by saying it's not anything bad; it's not a complaint or a problem.
- Thank her for agreeing to talk to you.
- Ask her directly: would she be willing to try to make things better between you, for everyone's sake?
- Tell her you know this might be difficult and scary for her, and you're nervous, too. Acknowledge that it might feel vulnerable and weird.
- You understand that the stressful aspects of the problems between you are hard *for both of you.*
- You just want to focus on handling one or two simple issues having to do with the kids so that things are manageable between you and so they don't escalate to bigger problems.
- You're not interested in "tackling" her with every known problem between you. You don't want to make her wrong. You're not looking to gain the upper hand.
- Ask if she'd be willing to take the same approach with you.
- Ask her if she would agree to take baby steps with you and go really slowly, at your own comfort levels.

If she's *not* interested or ready, then:

- Thank her for her time.
- Tell her you really don't want to keep the conflict going

between you two because it's too stressful, and you'll be trying to do things differently from here on out.

- Tell her you will respect her wishes to not talk about things now, but you hope she'll feel differently in the future.
- Let her know that you'd be willing to talk to her about this at any time, if she'd like.
- Exit the conversation in a polite and friendly way.
- If you're upset, talk to a supportive, understanding friend who won't turn this into a bigger drama with more conflict.

Set the stage and create a big picture for both of you

When you approach the other woman about a truce, *you* help set the parameters *for both of you*. Laying out the ground rules contributes to a feeling of safety and order.

In these contentious mother/stepmother relationships, you each have things you want, things you're afraid of, and an outcome you're hoping for. When you let her know you're not interested in tackling her to the ground verbally, or secretly trying to come out on top of the situation, she'll be more likely to meet you halfway. There are potentially a truckload of emotions and issues to cover here, but if you at least set in place some kind of protective foundation, you can take the time to do it gradually, with rests in between.

How you'd both like it to be

Let's imagine that the other woman is somewhat open to this scenario. Here's your chance to talk about some of the positive possibilities we covered in the last chapter. Create a visual picture for her of some of the benefits of you two getting along—for each person and for both families—better communication, less stress, being able to help each other with the kids, brainstorming solutions to parenting problems, etc. Ask her how she wishes it could be. Get her wheels spinning. Brainstorm together!

No blame/refusing to play "gotcha!"

You can't still be trying to "get" the other woman. You can't be trying to trap her and finally get her to see why she's "wrong." It will never happen, and certainly not *this* way. Realize that if you're fantasizing about being the top dog, you're still coming from a place of someone winning and someone losing. You've got to escape that mind-set and come back to a place of neutrality, a fresh start. When the lines of communication are stronger, *then* you can share stories of mutual dread and horror.

Have you ever had a big emotional breakthrough in a relationship with another person, whether friend, lover, family member, or coworker? You may have had some legitimate grievances, but at some point, you chose to set your objections aside. That's not to say you just blew your complaints off or made excuses for bad behavior. You simply understood that, eventually, there was a way to work around your points of contention—and then you shook hands with the other person, metaphorically or literally.

Can you do the same thing here? Maybe? Kinda? In increments?

Giving a little to get a lot

If there's something you know you've done wrong in your relationship, now's a good time to admit your mistakes and apologize for them, even if you do so a little at a time. Owning your own crap and saying you're sorry clears a path toward cooperation.

You may be thinking, *well, I'll only apologize if she apologizes too.* No such luck. You have no control over her behavior, but you do over yours. Your behavior is what you need to focus on for improving the situation between you two.

The art of apology

What is an apology, exactly?

It's a simple, *humble* statement about what you did wrong. You acknowledge that this is not how that person wants to be treated, nor how *you* want to treat her. You made a mistake, and you're human. An apology is an honest statement of regret or sorrow over your behavior, followed by a statement about how you intend to do things differently in the future.

The very last step is asking how you can make amends. You'd be surprised at how many people follow up an apology with justifications or rationalizations for what they've done, such as "I'm sorry, but here's why I did it, and why it wasn't my fault—" or "I only did it because you or someone else did _____." This has the effect of canceling out the apology!

When you apologize, you make yourself vulnerable and expose your weak spots. It's possible to do this truthfully and completely even in the face of hostility. You're apologizing for harm you've done to someone else as a way of making things right, and you're also making things right *inside you.*

No matter what kind of reaction you get from someone else, you can take pride in the fact that you're owning up to your errors and accepting responsibility. If your apology is real, the other person will know this on some level, even if she's trying to throw it back in your face.

You're still creating space for something to change between you, even if it happens later. Where are you with apologies in your life? How about a little game?

Quiz: Apology under a microscope

One of the best ways to say you're sorry:
  A. Screw. *You.*
  B. Yeah, I've probably done some things wrong, but taken a look at the mirror lately?
  C. It's not my fault that you've had such a hard time with things, I was only trying to be nice.
  D. Man oh man, I really messed up and I am truly sorry. How can I make it right?

If I apologize to her, I know she'll:
  A. Filet my soft underbelly, then eat me alive.
  B. Oh, she'll probably be nice to my face, and then she'll change her mind and use my words against me later.
  C. Just stay the same, mean self. I've tried and tried to say I'm sorry for things, but *she's* the one who just won't ever soften up.

D.   Probably want to make me wrong at first, but I also know the power of honesty and humility and I'm hopeful she'll come around.

Luckily,
A.   I never have to say I'm sorry because I never screw up.
B.   Sure, sometimes I make mistakes, but there's usually a good reason.
C.   I'm humble enough to see that I make mistakes all the time, and I'm always apologizing.
D.   I can say I'm sorry, even though it's grueling and sometimes humiliating, but I know I've done the right thing because I feel so much better afterward.

Scoring Guide

- If you answered mostly A's, you might want to work on reducing your anger.
- If you answered mostly B's, you've got the potential to be open and actually get somewhere, but perhaps you're only going halfway with your efforts. Keep going until the end.
- If you answered mostly C's, you may see yourself as a victim, which conveniently lets you off the hook. You may also be doing some counterproductive, passive-aggressive stuff. Experiment otherwise.
- If you answered mostly D's, bravo! You're well on your way to creating harmony with the other woman, and probably other people in your life, too.

STUFF TO KEEP IN MIND BEFOREHAND

Just a little reminder about why this is worth the pain in the ass . . .

In the United States, 1,400 new stepfamilies form every day! We can't afford to just leave stepmother/ex-wife relationships in the gutter. With the rate of divorce twice as high for remarried couples with children, there's too much at stake. Even if you're the ex-wife, do you want your children going through a second divorce? Probably not.

Here's a little reminder from Chapter Three: If you're willing to make the effort, even just a little bit at first, you stand to gain:

- less stress
- the relief and freshness of collaboration
- better parenting
- happier children
- friendship (maybe, eventually)
- less anger and bitterness in your life
- a stronger, more resilient relationship

It actually *is* possible to get along with someone you don't like. Even if you think you hate this person's guts, there's got to be *something* good about her. Can you think of at least three things? These are traits or characteristics you would savor if you two were friends. What would they be?

Now, changing tacks, what do you *respect* in her? What are her strong points? These might be different than the things you like about her, but would grudgingly admit are good qualities.

Spend a few moments thinking about this and see what you come up with. No one will have to know but you, so don't worry, your secrets are safe.

Communicate and act with accountability

We'll take a more in-depth look at communication and accountability in upcoming chapters. For now, we're just going to cover these two elements in broad terms. They deserve a mention since they have to do with the day-to-day ins and outs of living.

How do you *do* things with the other woman? Are you flaky? Are you on time? Do you "use your manners," even if you don't like her? Are you ever rude? Do you set her up to fail?

Do you make it a point to keep her up to date with all the various details about school and dental visits and colds and teen moodiness and lost notebooks and stuffed animals and whatever else is going on in the children's lives?

If you've got something to change or improve upon, do it, because it's the best way to keep a relationship running nice and clean, just like at work. You often have to work closely with folks you're not crazy about there—does that mean you're off the hook when it comes to doing a good job? Nope.

You can either be grim about the tasks before you, or you can dive in headlong with a shrug and a prayer and a sense of the many other women around you, all struggling with the same issues. Buddhists call it Big Mind. Knowing you're in good company helps you not feel so alone and can be a huge source of comfort and inspiration.

How about experimenting with something really simple?

How to greet the stepmom or ex-wife at the door when the kids swap houses
(Difficulty Level: Moderate to Difficult)

When the mom or stepmom comes to pick up the kids, it's usually . . . awkward. But with the right perspective and some good-behavior basics, it's totally doable.

Ingredients
- Children
- Any belongings the kids need to take with them
- A calm, can-do attitude
- Good manners

Instructions
- When the doorbell rings, lower the noise level in the house by turning down or turning off the TV or any music so you can easily hear and speak to each other.
- If you're on the phone, hang up. You can continue your conversation later.
- Put any barking or jumping dogs temporarily away.

- Take a deep breath before you turn the doorknob. Then take one more.
- Relax your face.
- As you open the door, smile! Make eye contact.
- Ask the stepmom or mom to come in and make eye contact again. Be warm, if possible.
- Make chitchat: ask her about traffic, the weather, etc. (If there's something specific you know she's been doing, follow up on that to let her know that you pay attention to the things she's interested in.)
- Invite her to sit down if the kids are being slow.
- If you feel uncomfortable, try to imagine that you're talking to a neighbor you don't know very well. You would still be polite and friendly, right?
- If there's any information you need to communicate to her, do that now (homework deadlines, medical or dental appointments, illnesses, playdates, etc.). Write information down if need be.
- When everyone is ready to go, say goodbye to the kids. Say something simple and encouraging about their upcoming time together ("Enjoy your new book! Have a good time at ___!"). You want the kids to feel optimistic about making the transition to the other house. If they see that you're calm and agreeable, it will help them develop the same perspective.
- Make sure to say goodbye to the stepmother or ex-wife as well; addressing her by name is a nice touch. Make eye contact again.
- Gently close the door.
- Take a deep breath. Then take another one.

Tips & Notes
- Be prepared. Make sure the kids have packed up beforehand and their things are ready by the door. Help them if they need it.

- Talk to the kids beforehand about not dawdling so you don't keep the stepmom or mom waiting.
- Don't worry about how clean your house is compared to their house. This is a contest no one will ever win.

A note to moms: Even if you don't like the stepmother, she'll be taking care of your children for a set period of time, so you want to set the right tone with her from the very beginning, for the kids' sake. If the children see you interacting with the stepmother with courtesy and respect, you convey the message that you expect the same behavior from them.

If the children misbehave toward the stepmother, nip any bad behavior in the bud immediately. Take them aside privately and let them know that this person is to be treated with consideration, no matter what. Not liking someone is no excuse to let manners fly out the window.

A note to stepmoms: Even if you don't like the mother (or the kids!), do your best to keep the feeling in the air positive and clear. Not liking someone is no excuse to just toss your manners in the dumpster.

If you're having difficulties with the stepchildren, try not to transpose your feelings of frustration and anger (especially potential judgments about her parenting skills if you believe they are contributing to your problems) onto the mom. If you've got a beef with the mom, see if you can take it up with her privately. Take things one experience at a time.

SIGNALING A SEA CHANGE

Let's take a closer look at some things you can try to show the other woman that there's a change in the air. Lucky for you, you have lots of options. Pick the one that most appeals and fits best. Shoot for a nice mixture of risk and comfort.

Send her an e-mail
Before you stick your neck out in person or on the phone, you might want to try sending her an e-mail. Forward something hilarious or

touching, or related to one of her interests. Perhaps you could send her a link to our Web site or other Web sites devoted to improving relationships between mothers and stepmothers (there are only a few out there; we've listed them at the end of the first chapter).

Send her a card

Everyone likes getting mail. Plus, these days, personal mail is about as rare as a pen when you need one. If you'd like to give the other woman something she can treasure forever (or something tangible to burn), then a heartfelt card is the way to go. You can buy something funny, beautiful, or sappy enough to require cursive writing.

Talk on the phone

You might start here, just to establish a more personal touch. Think about it: You can quickly get away; you're in your own protected space; and you can compose yourself beforehand. She can hear you laugh (or cry), but she can't hear your heart going a hundred beats per minute or see you sweating profusely.

A small gift or offering, with no strings attached

Is there something you could send to her or actually take her that you think she might like? A great read? A bar of decadent chocolate? A CD that you burned or bought? Something you baked for her? Some craft item you made for her?

When you bring someone a gift, you communicate to her primitive brain: Okay, this person is making an effort with me. Perhaps I still don't trust her, but I will leave a tiny opening there and see what happens.

INVITE HER FOR COFFEE

This deserves its own special category. If you're feeling brave and prefer the one-on-one intimacy of meeting in person, you could start here. You have the biggest chance of making true progress face-to-face, but you also run the greatest risk of ending up in an argument. A meeting is not for the reckless or faint of heart. Move gradually with safer contact beforehand to ensure the greatest chances of success.

If you're going to meet in person, there are a few guiding principles to follow:

1. Work on her subconscious trust of you

Pay attention to how you're conducting yourself, things like words and semantics, tone of voice, body language, and eye contact.

Are your arms crossed in front of you, like you're angry or defensive? Even if you're only doing this because you're nervous, be conscious of the kind of message your body posture might be sending.

Be careful about blaming language too. Phrases such as "you always—" or "you never—" or "well, that was because you—" will set off the other person's alarms in a big way and make her feel as if she's under attack. We use these phrases because *we* already feel blamed somehow and are trying to shift that burden away to the other person. But inflammatory language only makes the situation worse.

When you look into her face, see if you can soften your eyes and the muscles in your face. Again, you may be incredibly nervous, but think about what you want her to see when she looks at you: someone who's open, who's actually listening to her, who cares about doing things differently, and who is trying to make a real and honest connection with her.

Pretend your way into good behavior. Even if you're not feeling it, push yourself to be upbeat, to seem warm and friendly. Sometimes, when we push ourselves a little bit, we can actually help ourselves *get there* and the next thing you know, you actually do feel better.

2. How to listen to her while she's talking

Actually *listen* to the words coming out of her mouth, instead of the argument taking place inside your head. Try to understand her *meaning*.

Pretend you're going to be tested on the main points of her conversation. Pay attention and take them in, even if you don't agree with them.

Play the Double Feelings Game. Identify what feelings seem to be going along with what she's saying, both at a surface level and at a deeper level, where those feelings might be hidden. For instance, she may be saying something to you in an angry way, but underneath, feel scared and threatened. "Listen" for both levels in other areas of your life as well so you can get really good at this, and watch your relationships blossom.

Summarize what she just told you before you move on to another subject. Ask her if you have it right. Verify.

Create a transition between what you understood her to be saying and what you'd like to say regarding that same issue. Hopefully, she will listen more carefully to *you* if she feels as if she's been heard herself.

3. Work on one issue at a time

If you actually *do* establish a connection with the mom or stepmom and start to get excited about being able to work together, take note: *simplicity is your friend.* Try to work on *only one* issue at a time, instead of *everything* that's going wrong, like this is your only chance to get anywhere.

Remember what it's like in a romantic partnership when you're trying to resolve one problem and your partner brings up three others that seem completely unrelated? That's what makes people want to give up.

It's tricky, because often one issue does lead to another. Maybe your child or stepchild is having problems doing his or her homework (Problem No. 1) because the child is watching too much TV (Problem No. 2) or hanging out online too much (Problem No. 3). How do you handle tackling Problem No. 1 without dragging the other two problems into the picture? Maybe the child watches too much TV because he or she is home alone after school, or one adult has different limits about TV and lets him or her watch more than the other side feels comfortable with. This is very common, and it's hard to go backward with a problem without eventually getting to a problem that seems to point directly at someone else. Not comfortable.

So what do you do?

Keep it straightforward and simple. Identify *one* manageable problem that's potentially resolvable. Something that has to do with:

- pickups and drop-offs
- meals
- bedtime and sleeping
- friends and playdates
- homework
- TV or Internet or video game usage

Try your best to continue to keep the focus on the actual problem itself. For example, you could simply bring the conversation back to the child's homework situation and their grades. "Yes, I understand you have to bring work home from the office, and it's difficult to monitor the kids' TV time, but how can we help them get back on track with their schoolwork? What can we do?"

4. What to actually say to each other

Remember what we talked about initially when asking for a truce? Plug in some of the same pieces again here:

- Thank her for agreeing to meet you.
- Acknowledge the fact that this might be difficult or scary and tell her you feel nervous, too.
- Say something about your hopes for how things could be between you if you could remove and/or contain some of the difficult behavior you've both struggled with in the past. Plant a positive vision in her mind and use it to guide your behavior, too.
- Watch the language: avoid "you never," "you always," and "well, that's because you_____," or "well, if only you'd done ___, then ____ wouldn't have happened."
- Throw it out there in plain language: I won't blame you, please don't blame me.
- Work on one or two simple parenting goals.
- Plan a time to follow up.

5. All the stars in the dark sky

Don't forget to remind yourself of all the good that's awaiting you here: a brand-new version of cooperation and teamwork; a brighter future for the kids as you make their lives smoother and more organized and integrated; less bitching and moaning in your relationship and with friends; and lower levels of stress and angst.

You might actually get along! It's possible! Get excited!

6. Focus on the children/stepchildren

This is important! Don't talk poorly about the children to each other, even if you need to vent. You might bond a bit over shared frustrations, but you don't want to say anything you'll feel guilty about later (or that could come back to haunt you).

If you two decide to work on a problem having to do with the children, take it one step at a time and don't overwhelm the kids with a bunch of changes all at once. They may feel uncomfortable with this if they can't figure out what's going on, or feel ganged up on. Take it slow.

Make sure to practice the same rules for non-gossip about the mom or stepmom *with* the kids. (There's more about gossip in Chapter Seven.)

EXTRA REASSURANCE

Hanging by your nails off a cliff

If you're flailing here, just know this step is one of the hardest parts of this process—it's perfectly natural to struggle, to feel overwhelmed, to not have it go like it does in the movies. At least time is on your side, because you'll have *plenty* of opportunities to keep experimenting.

Plus, the old adage that people never change is not true—people *do* change. You know that because you've done it yourself.

And see—really, it didn't work!

So what if you reach out, heart and soul dangling by a thread, and she basically throws it all back in your face? There's a psychological technique where you imagine the worst possible scenario all the way to its bitter end and then ask yourself: Would this kill me? Could I get over this? Can I pick myself back up and move on and eventually let this go? Do the same thing here.

Let's say you end up in an argument. She hauls out her whole laundry list of your offenses, your mistakes, and flaming failures. She couldn't give a damn about any stupid truce. The words "friend" and "(insert your name here)" will never be linked together in a million years if she can help it. Matter of fact, YOU are a total idiot for even trying! Probably you're only doing so because you *know* how wrong you are in the first place and you feel guilty, with all the shenanigans you've pulled.

Well, we sigh with you as you're sighing. These things happen.

And . . .

It is perfectly *possible* to pick yourself up, brush yourself off, and regroup. You're going to be fine.

Take some deep breaths in the car. Listen to music you love. Get though the immediate moments afterward and emphasize to yourself that she has her issues, you have yours, and you're each responsible for handling your own garbage.

Call a supportive friend, but make sure it's the right one. Meaning, someone who's willing to listen with a neutral ear and call you on your self-righteous shit if need be. Someone who understands your overall goals of wanting partnership and harmony, and will wend their way through your emotions with that outcome in mind.

Go exercise to blow off steam and release negative energy.

Meditate, watch mindless TV. Do whatever it takes to let go . . . .

This is going to be the last thing you want to hear, but at some point, you may be ready to try again.

Rinse, lather, repeat.

You may have your doubts about whether it's possible to establish any sense of cooperation and communication with the other woman. But before you bound onto the Bandwagon of Scorn, ask yourself if you're taking the easy way out. A lot of stepmoms and ex-wives hate each other. And most women are happy to just leave it at that, convinced it's really the other side's fault.

See if you can give it another go—another time. Give yourself some space to settle back into yourself; adopt the Zen discipline of a no-gossip policy; follow up on anything you said you would.

Practice doesn't always make perfect. But actions taken from a place of humility and good intentions always have their own inherent, rewarding grace.

Quiz: What changes am I willing to make?

What would you be willing to try? What actions appeal to you? Rate the various possibilities and make a plan to take action including a target timeline for making it happen.

Say hello to her differently										
Overall willingness:	1	2	3	4	5	6	7	8	9	10
What I plan to do:										

Greet her at the door differently										
Overall willingness:	1	2	3	4	5	6	7	8	9	10
What I plan to do:										

Send her an e-mail										
Overall willingness:	1	2	3	4	5	6	7	8	9	10
What I plan to do:										

Send her a card or letter										
Overall willingness:	1	2	3	4	5	6	7	8	9	10
What I plan to do:										

Talk to her on the phone										
Overall willingness:	1	2	3	4	5	6	7	8	9	10
What I plan to do:										

Give her a small gift										
Overall willingness:	1	2	3	4	5	6	7	8	9	10
What I plan to do:										

Invite her for coffee										
Overall willingness:	1	2	3	4	5	6	7	8	9	10
What I plan to do:										

RESOURCES TO EXPLORE

Books

- *The Art of Forgiveness, Lovingkindness, and Peace,* by Jack Kornfield
- *The Shelter of Each Other: Rebuilding Our Families,* by Mary Pipher, Ph.D.
- *The Five Things We Cannot Change and the Happiness We Find by Embracing Them,* by David Richo

Web sites

- Forgiving (www.forgiving.org)
- Pick the Brain (www.pickthebrain.com)
- Wild Mind - Buddhist Meditation (www.wildmind.org)

AS WE LEAVE THE CHAPTER

Try out some new behaviors and see what happens. But remember, experimentation is not a one-time thing—you'll be coming back to these same techniques again and again.

If you need some extra encouragement during this process, leap ahead to Chapter Eight: Regroup, and get yourself back to a place where you feel centered and calm. Or jump back to Chapter Three: Imagine the Benefits, and see if you can sharpen your focus on your goals.

Then try something different when you feel ready.

The rewards are worth it. And the relief of gradually leaving all that negative stuff behind will be palpable.

Next, we'll be learning about how to successfully add the element of cooperation into the mix.

5

Collaborate

(Lighten Your Load—and Hers)

NO SINGING, JUST DRENCHED

*Ironically, this chapter was one of the hardest for us to write. You'd think if we were capable of writing this book, we'd be singing the praises of collaboration from the rooftops **together**, in three-part harmony. But the truth is, we had an abundance of false starts, many misunderstandings, and plenty of outright failures in our attempts to problem-solve in tandem. Now that we have the benefit of hindsight, we more clearly understand **why**, and one of the primary causes came as a surprise even to us! We'll try to help you avoid some of the mistakes we made.*

A LOOK BACK FROM US

Carol: My oldest stepdaughter, S., lived with us for a year when she was about fourteen. It was a trying year for me, to say the least. She and I had always gotten along fairly well before, but she was right at that age in a teen's life when adults are clearly inferior human beings and none of us "understand anything at all!"

My task that year was to pick her up from school every day. She was going to a magnet school about fifteen minutes away from the house and in the beginning, it worked out well.

However, as the year wore on, we said less and less to each other in the car. Whatever I said (even if it was simply "Hey, how was your day?") was somehow me interrogating or lecturing her and she didn't take to it kindly. Our interactions in the car each day also mirrored life at home, except there, she could escape to her room.

When she first came to live with us, I set down some ground rules. They were fairly simple and, I thought, reasonable. She needed to clean up any messes, especially in the kitchen. She had to ask me before she used my things. And there were no food or drinks allowed up in her room.

Each time a rule was broken there was a consequence. I tried taking away allowance—she didn't care. I tried taking away computer/TV time—she didn't care. I tried grounding her for a weekend—she cared, a lot. But it was only toward the end of the year that I discovered this!

One day I was taking clean laundry up to her room and discovered food everywhere. There were several brown bags full of the half-eaten lunches I made for her every morning—in the trash, rotting.

I started to fume. Why did she do this when I specifically asked her not to? Was this a personal attack, or was she just being lazy?! Did she not believe me when I said there would be a consequence? She didn't even try to hide it!

I paced. I considered my options. And then I called my husband at work and talked it over with him. She had been warned about food in her room countless times; it was time to crack down with a bigger consequence. So I said I was going to ground her for the weekend. He said fine.

Then I called Jennifer and she had the same response. I was going to tell S. on the way home from school.

Within the hour, I got two phone calls with the same message. One from David and one from Jennifer, both saying they'd thought it over and both (separately) thought my punishment was too harsh.

I thought they were being big weenies. This has been my main complaint about them both as parents: They're too inconsistent about following through with consequences because . . . well, I don't really know why! But, in my opinion, I think it's led to a confusing atmosphere of discipline and both kids breaking rules a lot more often.

So I asked Jennifer and David for alternate suggestions and one of them (I don't remember who) suggested taking away her allowance for the month instead. We had an arrangement at the time that she got fifty dollars a month. But she had to budget that amount and pay for all her own clothes, books, music, shoes, toiletries, school supplies, trips with friends, etc. I even thought *this* punishment was a bit much myself, but decided to offer both as alternatives.

I gave S. a choice on the way home from school. She chose to lose the allowance without even thinking about it. I was happy that at *least* there was a consequence and we followed through with it, even though, in hindsight, grounding her might have been more effective. Unfortunately, we still had issues with food in the room afterward. And soon after that, she moved back in with her mom, in part I think because I was threatening to ground her for other things. It was really stressful.

I had many altercations with my stepdaughter that year, and despite our differences in opinion, it was such a relief to be able to confer with Jennifer about how to handle them.

After S. moved back to the other house, Jennifer called me fairly often, as she struggled with a lot of the same issues. It was nice to have some common ground—to be able to say, "Yep, I understand, we had the same kind of argument here before and it hurt like hell," or "Well, this is how we handled it, and that seemed to work."

Jennifer: Recently, I babysat David and Carol's three-year old son, J., for a full weekend. I offered to watch both him and their two standard poodles in exchange for some badly needed Web design work. I felt up to the job, as long as the girls were here.

I was so proud of my two daughters and how much they helped out. Of course, they each have their own relationship to J. since he's their brother, but I got a closer look at what that's all about.

When he was crying repeatedly throughout his first night here, it was my oldest daughter, S. (then sixteen), who got up with me the first three or four times without complaint. She held J. to soothe him; she even crawled into his crib at one point to help him fall asleep. "Don't worry, I've done this before," she assured me. That crib sure seemed awfully small!

M. (then twelve) in particular really knows J. especially well, now that she's living with her dad and stepmom. She babysits him twice a week while Carol paints and takes her (paying) job very seriously. She was able to handily advise me on matters of food and sleep preferences, but was thrilled to be able to leave the dirty diaper changes to me.

I enjoyed sitting with J. alone on the couch, pulling out our tattered little-kid books, which haven't been looked at in eons. I improvised with the words to keep his attention, rediscovering some of my favorite picture books all over again. I watched him hunt for animals hidden in trees, study odd visual details, and relished hearing him repeat my words after me in his cute high voice.

J. didn't ask for his parents too much during the day. I think it helped that, along with his two big sisters, his two big dogs were here too, knocking up against him. It was like part of his house just migrated over here with him.

The hardest part of the whole weekend was Saturday night.

Friday night had been hell, with J. waking up over and over and over (I lost track around the tenth time, so it's all a blur). Every time he cried hard, I went in to soothe him. Saturday morning, I was a wreck and so was he. He couldn't seem to nap that afternoon, but the girls watched over him while I slept.

At the urgent (and guilty) advice of David and Carol all the way from Dallas, I was to let him cry it out on Saturday night. This was a routine they already had in their house and it worked pretty well, with J. knowing what to expect and rarely fussing for long. I was more of an attachment parenting kind of mom when the girls were younger, but at this point in my life, I think there's something to be said for either school. I would try their approach out of respect for them, and selfishly, so that I could get some more sleep.

Nevertheless, it was pretty grueling to hear him crying and yelling my name from the other room. "Help me, Jen!" "Jen! Help me!" I finally called David and Carol again for reassurance. How long should I do this? What if he never stopped crying? I felt terrible!

Eventually, thankfully . . . he settled down. I kept waking up, thinking I'd heard him cry, but when I got out of bed . . . silence.

The next morning, I realized the windows to his room had been *open* (though the room had been warm enough). Great! Now the neighbors were all going to think I had been flogging him the night before. But J. was fine and seemingly unscathed, happy, and chipper. It was funny—our two approaches to parenting had each had their turn.

One of my very favorite memories was sitting around the dinner table together in the evening. We have four chairs at the table and there's usually one or more chairs empty at dinner. Little J. was right there, perched on a pillow and a towel, chomping away, spiking his food deliberately with a fork. All of our chairs were full . . . .

It felt complete and right, having J. here, like he was family visiting—which he was. And knowing we got to give Carol and David a weekend off alone made me feel really good.

You just never know what's going to happen in these new extended families once they're up and running.

A CLOSER LOOK AT COLLABORATION

Why it's necessary

We cannot parent in isolation. We need each other. Whether the father is also a hands-on parent or not, there will probably be times when the stepmother and mom will need to bail each other out. Imagine if you could count on the other woman to brainstorm stubborn problems, to provide a fresh perspective or solutions you may not have considered. Couldn't we all use another pair of hands? Another brain?

We know it might still seem impossible to establish a connection between the two of you if you've just begun to experiment with actions from the last chapter. Perhaps things are still tense between you and you feel bogged down by negative residue from past experiences. This is perfectly natural, even expected. Would it help you to know we're not shooting for perfection?

Give and take

Collaboration is a *dance;* it's ongoing, evolving, a process. You don't reach some solid state of "achievement" with the other person and then, *boom,* you're done. We *still* have to do the back-and-forth tango with each other, and even all these years later, it's sometimes tricky to talk about touchy subjects.

The range of experiences here is huge, with many potential failures, but an even wider scope of possibilities. You may end up being simply business partners who logically and factually discuss certain aspects of taking care of the children. You might end up becoming cordial friends, or even close friends.

Even if there's little progress made toward actual warmth between you, perhaps you'll at least begin to minimize the more contentious aspects of your relationship. You might still be nervous dealing with each other. You may discover, upon closer inspection—nope—you still don't necessarily like the other person. That's okay. You're not setting out to be best friends forever. You just want to handle the numerous details of your parenting lives without declaring war against each other.

How it was hard for us

We have v-e-r-y different styles in many of the colliding aspects of our lives. We've already referred in earlier chapters to differences we have over parenting, consequences, and discipline, over organization and routines. And especially detailed differences of opinion over how to cultivate self-discipline in the children.

We have lots of stories about how we tried to talk through various parenting issues, only to end up frustrated at where the conversation was going, which seemed to be blame or frustration with the other side. It's hard to keep talking when that hits you, and it's hard to keep listening!

Both of us have really "given" during some of those conversations, and we've both refused to budge an inch. What made some of those talks even harder was the fact that, actually, the other person was sometimes *right*. We both hate to admit that, but it's true. The other person was taking note of our mistakes, our blind spots, and, of course, those are also our sore spots. We realize now that those were qualities and shortcomings that were (and most likely, still are) underdeveloped and needed work.

Nevertheless, we keep plugging away because we're stubborn—we complement each other in that way.

Some problems went away because the kids outgrew some of their issues, despite what we did. Some issues we actually managed to successfully tackle together, and there were some thorny topics that we really struggled with and *still* haven't figured out.

Who? Just two?

Who's going to be in on this process? Just you two, or the father too? If he seems amenable, you may want to invite him to team up with you. Or you might just want to focus on the relationship between the two of you to make it simpler and easier. If the father feels that he *must* participate in order to support what the two of you are creating, then by all means, figure out a way to make him feel included. You could discuss some things by e-mail in which all parties are copied, you could have a conference call, you could do the primitive thing and actually meet face-to-face.

DEFENSIVENESS

The key to it all

Defensiveness is one of the most critical barriers between you and harmonious cooperation. You must clear the hurdle of defensiveness to be able to collaborate with the other person. Many of the problems you encounter as you attempt to work together can likely be attributed to this one contentious element.

Have you ever been venting about a family member (for convenience, we'll call them FM) to a friend, partner, or more distant family member? Even if you were complaining about the same person one moment before, it's another thing altogether to have your listener jump in and do it, too. Something instinctive and protective kicks in and a part of you immediately leaps to the defense of FM, no matter how frustrated you might otherwise be with FM.

Why does this happen? Because you feel closely linked or aligned with FM. Suddenly, it seems as if whatever the other person is saying about FM, he or she is saying about *you*. Their words are a reflection of your self-worth, your effectiveness in some area or another, your entire lineage! Your reaction is swift, knee-jerk, and seems automatic: You feel indignant, insulted, and vaguely ashamed. You cannot seem to separate the words from the offended feelings.

Tread with care!

This mirroring effect is magnified *tenfold* when it comes to our children or how we are perceived as caretakers and parents. Let's see what this looks like in each woman.

From the mother's perspective: You don't want anyone else saying *anything negative* about your child or children. Period. If they do, there's a good chance you'll just cut short the conversation or change the subject. Somewhere in the back of your mind, you might put a little tick mark next to that person's name and subtly think of them as an enemy to your family.

From the stepmother's perspective: You don't want anyone insinuating that you're not doing a good job parenting your stepchildren. If they seem to be pointing out an area where you're struggling with judgment or criticism, you know you'll never be confiding in *them* again. It's even harder to parent children that aren't your own!

Survey: Push my buttons and I'll deck you

What are your "buttons"? What are your fearful sore spots when it comes to being a parent or having stepchildren? See if you can relate to the worries below. Do you have any unique variations on these themes, hidden away?

Use a set of colored pencils or colored markers or just a pen or pencil if that's all you have. For each statement, fill in the bar to rate your level of concern, as shown in the sample scale.

Here's a sample scale:

Less intense   In the middle   Almost unbearable

1. I worry that I'm not a good enough parent/stepparent.

2. I feel like I never spend enough time with the kids.

3. I have a bad temper; I'm too easily angry.
   _____

4. I struggle with being a perfectionist.
   _____

5. I know I'm an inconsistent authority figure.
   _____

6. I'm always spread too thin/overwhelmed.
   _____

7. I'm not doing this as well as the other woman.
   _____

8. I'm too much of a pushover with the kids.
   _____

9. Uh . . . I guess you could say I have control issues.
   _____

10. I'm too involved in/distracted by other things.
    _____

Read on for some new ideas on how to talk about difficult subjects without getting "activated."

A definite impact

What are the consequences of being defensive? Think of defensiveness as the rope that ties your hands together, making it impossible for you to resolve your problems. When one or both women are defensive and feel attacked, suddenly what either party is "allowed" to say in the conversation shrinks dramatically. You cannot speak the truth. You have to walk on eggshells. You have to talk *around* the problem, instead of naming it directly. You feel as if you're biting your tongue. All of this just adds to your frustration with the original problem itself, and now you probably feel paralyzed and resentful on top of it.

How to work through your own defensiveness

When you're defensive, you assume that someone is attacking you now for something you or your loved one did in the past, and you're anticipating more attacks in the future. It's all too easy to handle conflict this way and, for many of us, the habit is so ingrained we don't even see it as an issue.

The remedy is to try your hardest to simply focus on the matter at hand and deal with *that.* Change your perspective. Separate the problem from the person giving you feedback and from what you think the problem means about *you,* because they are two separate and different things. What can you do to help resolve these challenges at this moment—or in the immediate future?

You may not have figured out the solutions yet, but they are there, waiting to be discovered. And it's easier to find solutions if you have help looking.

THE AMAZING POWER OF "JUST TALKING"

Start out by simply opening the door to a dialogue with the other person—*and actually listen!* Engaging in a genuine dialogue can potentially have enormous benefits. When you're struggling and need help, or just don't know what to do, it can be such a relief to turn to the other person for support, understanding, and validation. Encourage the other person to do the same with you. Just feeling *heard* by the other person can feel very comforting, whether you come up with a resolution to your problems or not. Think about the many times someone has said the following phrases to you and made you feel better:

- "Yeah, that was horrible!"
- "I know exactly what you mean. One time I . . . ."
- "What if you tried doing (helpful idea)?"
- "I did (helpful idea) before and this happened (positive results)."

Here are some things *not* to do during a dialogue:
- Blame the other person's style or parenting habits as the source for the problem.
- Ask the other person to make really sweeping or unrealistic changes.

- Put your philosophy or style forth as the obviously superior one.
- Say you're going to do something and then not do it.

What to actually DO during a dialogue to increase your chances of success:
- Listen to the other person; let her finish and have her say.
- Show the other person you're *trying* to understand her perspective.
- If you can sympathize with her anger, her hurt feelings, or her frustration, relay a similar experience, or just say so.
- See if you can come up with any fresh ideas that might help solve the problem, even a little bit.
- Invite her to work on this with you: *Would you be willing to see if we can figure this out together?*
- Use respectful language.
- Put aside your own reaction as best you can and explain your position after the other person has said her piece completely.
- Don't defend your own choices as if someone is right and someone is wrong; just *listen*.

(See Chapter Four for more ideas on how to defuse a difficult conversation and reduce the potential for arguments.)

Establish common ground

Rather than trying to tackle everything at once, determine a starting point between you, an area where you both share some common values or concerns. Figure out what's compatible about your styles and go from there. Leave the harder stuff for later. You can always come back to it when you've established a firmer foundation beneath your partnership. For now, just put the rest on the back burner.

The benefit to this approach is you get to focus on a topic where you can actually make some headway. For us, even when we couldn't agree on many ideas about discipline exactly, we at least supported each other with imposing punishments that carried over from house to house.

List the ideas that are popping up in your head as you read this section. Are you starting to get a sense of the possibilities for collaborating with the other woman?

_____

_____

_____

_____

_____

_____

_____

_____

_____

WHAT ABOUT THE MAN?

The question here should be: *How can you get your ex-husband or husband to help you?* How can you enroll him in your quest to create harmony, between the two of you first, and then between both families? How can you address his fears? Have a conversation and ask him what he thinks about the whole idea. Ask him about his concerns and then do your best to allay them.

But first, the stepmother and the mother each have their own unique challenges when it comes to collaborating with the father of the children. The element of "baggage" rears its ugly head again, interfering with the creation of a sense of partnership in all directions.

Stepmoms and their husbands

The stepmother may find that her husband also suffers from a severe case of knee-jerk defensiveness when it comes to the children. This can lead to the same sorts of complications that were outlined above: The stepmother feels like she's walking on eggshells and can't just talk about the issues plainly. That means that she also can't fully address the problems that *do* exist with the stepchildren. Instead of venting freely about her feelings, her frustrations, and perhaps her own critical opinions in a difficult situation, she must choose her words carefully and perhaps even censor herself.

Otherwise, conversations about the stepchildren may lead to arguments, anger, and an abundance of hurt feelings in both directions. Carol has said that she didn't fully understand David's automatic defensiveness about his children until she had a child herself, and then it made perfect sense. If anyone ever seemed to inadvertently criticize her child, she could feel the same protective, volatile feelings immediately flare up in her.

Mothers and ex-husbands

Both the ex-husband and the mother likely feel defensive with each other about their parenting, in some way. They may each feel as if the other person blames them for behaviors in the children that are not *their* fault. They may each feel completely stumped when it comes to resolving certain problems and yet feel as if the other parent is still waiting for them to do so.

The leftover baggage from the split will influence how supportive he feels, how willing he is to work on things. We've said it before, but if you're the ex-wife, we encourage you to do whatever you can to let go of old grievances between you two and heal your relationship. Not only will this encourage collaboration directly with him, but it can greatly influence your relationship with the stepmother.

It can also be different between the exes, as compared to the stepmom and mom. If they've already healed some of the hurt feelings between them, it may be possible for them to talk about problems the kids are having together without triggering defensiveness on either side. Once Jennifer saw that Carol was in the picture for the long haul, it became easier for her to feel less critical toward Carol and less like Carol was waiting for her to fail as a parent, particularly when she saw her struggling, too.

Father Guilt

If the father is not the custodial parent, he may suffer from guilt that also affects his ability to see any "fault" in his children. It's particularly hard for him to focus on their shortcomings if he hasn't seen them in a while or doesn't get to spend much time with them because of his schedule. He doesn't want to seem like the bad guy when they come over. This fear can be remedied by creating some consistency between the households, which we discuss below.

CONSISTENT RULES BETWEEN HOUSES

The benefits of consistency

When the rules and punishments are the same between both houses, something funny starts to happen. It's harder for kids to misbehave! They can't act up, get in trouble, and then, *whoops*, they're going off to Dad's or Mom's house and now the punishment dissolves, whether it's complete or not. They stop trying to *negotiate* different rules with you because the rules are that much harder to change. There's less wiggle room. And kids know where they stand and what they can expect.

There's a good chance they're not going to like this (we know ours didn't), but it certainly makes parenting easier. You have someone else reinforcing the changes you're trying to make because there's more family stability and a more seamless sense of authority all around. Everyone wins.

Here are some ways that we've collaborated in the past and still do:
- Calling each other, asking for the other person's take on the situation.
- Venting to each other about hurt feelings, or being frustrated and out of patience, angry.
- Planning with each other for birthdays and holidays—what to cook or make, presents to buy, helping each other figure out what the children want.
- Meeting each other halfway when it comes to pickups or drop-offs so that the other person doesn't have to drive the whole way (we live about thirty minutes away from each other). We take turns driving if one person drives the whole way.

- Imposing punishments that are unfinished when the child comes back to your house, even if you disagree with the punishment. (We talk about that in private.)
- Experimenting with new rules for allowances, chores, rules for bedtime, curfew, etc.

The beginning of brainstorming

So where can you start with the other person? Look around at your own life and see if there are some simple things the other woman could help you with that would make a big difference. Are you aware of areas where she is struggling and could also use a hand? What do the kids complain about when they come home? For example, if one child is not eating a lot of vegetables at home, you could ask for help in figuring out which ones the child is willing to eat (in our house, it's spinach, broccoli, corn, and carrots). That's a very basic example, but we recommend starting out simple, even if you have teenagers, and build upon your successes from there.

Take a moment to look through the list below and then answer a few questions in preparation for your upcoming conversation.

- Back and forth between houses
- Discipline and consequences
- Responsibility and chores
- School and homework
- TV and computer time
- Allowance
- Playdates
- Bad behavior
- Meals and health

JOURNAL

What rules and consequences would you like to see created for the topics above? Are there any areas that seem to be in particular need of action or attention? What rules are negotiable or flexible for you? Which ones are non-negotiable?

So what would a conversation about these things look like in action? We've outlined a possible sequence for the discussion below. Again, remember to start out in an area that you have in common with the other woman, if possible.

How to ask someone for her help
- Greet her as warmly as you can.
- Let her know you have a problem that you'd like to get her feedback on and support with.
- Ask her if she'd be willing to help.
- Explain the situation in as neutral a language as possible (remember the phrases to avoid in the last chapter: "You always—", "You never—", "If only you would or wouldn't— ").
- Explain which parts of the situation you're most concerned about or need the most help with. You might explain some of the options you're weighing or explain why you feel torn between different ideas.
- Ask her for her feedback or any possible solutions.
- When she gives you her feedback, do your best to hear what she's saying, instead of reacting.
- Reflect her ideas back to her to make sure you understand what she's saying. See if you can blend your ideas and hers to come up with a combined solution.
- If you're struggling, let her know where your sticking points are, explain your fears and concerns.
- If her concerns are similar to what she's said before and you want to roll your eyes, take a deep breath. Consider for a moment if there might be any validity to what she's saying.
- Acknowledge her efforts to help you come up with a solution.
- If you are going to try out any of her ideas, let her know this, or tell her you'd like to think about it a bit more before making a decision.
- Tell her you'll let her know how it goes.
- Even if you don't feel that you've come away from the conversation with something new or helpful, make sure to clearly *thank her for her time and ideas.*

Talking to the kids about new rules

So let's say the meeting is successful and you each come up with a few new ideas you're going to try around the house. Here are a few things to keep in mind:

NO BOMBARDMENTS

Don't do what we did and have a big meeting where you pounce on the kids and let them know about all the things they're doing wrong! (We still cringe at this memory.) We started off our first meeting with a bang, and it ended in tears all the way around. Not pretty. We felt emboldened by being a united front, thinking this would make certain messages sink in, but in reality, we only ended making the kids feel scared, wrong, and as if we were ganging up on them.

BREAK CHANGES TO THE KIDS GENTLY

Start with simple things. Let them know that these new rules are going to apply at both houses from now on. Tell them explicitly what will happen if they don't follow the rules. Follow through (this is important!). Let them know all the adults are going to be communicating with each other about how this goes, and you're all expecting them to try their best, too.

YIN AND YANG

Make sure to balance new rules and consequences for misbehavior with chances for family fun and bonding (see Chapter Nine for more ideas). Do something fun with the kids and go out to dinner together, all of you. Or go out for ice cream, to the park, or the movies—let them choose.

Show the kids what it looks like for former adversaries to be getting along, and be prepared for them to stand there with their mouths hanging open. Be proud of yourself for doing something unusual and generous, with someone you still may not even like. (But we bet you're getting closer . . . .)

A fact worth emphasizing: You're at the very *beginning* of mending your families; this can be the start of a whole new, stronger family unit.

Take care of it, and treat it with respect, just like you would a fledgling sprout.

EXTRA REASSURANCE

Release your agenda

What if you feel like you're *still* totally working against each other? Here's a crazy idea you can try that just might work.

Author Harville Hendrix has a novel approach for working through conflict with another person: *Make the other person's needs your priority, instead of your own.* This may sound like the exact opposite of what you want, but that's the whole point. For a moment, put yourself in the other person's shoes and try to understand *why* she wants *what* she wants. It's also an opportunity for you to see if you are operating from any blind spots or places inside *you* that need to grow. Remember earlier in the chapter where we talked about this? What are some of your potential blind spots? Are your buttons getting pushed? Change your focus and see what happens.

Prioritize your top three concerns

You might also be trying to do too much. Go back to simplicity and identify your top three concerns, rated by their level of priority. What really needs to be worked on now? What can wait until a bit later? What can wait even longer? Pick your battles and don't waste your efforts. And remember, there is such a thing as *good enough*. You do your best, then you shrug the rest off and let the chips fall where they may. What does "good enough" look like for you? What modicum of cooperation would you be happy with? In that spirit, let's drill down to some concrete ideas for improvement.

Quiz: Help me! And how can I help you?

What are some ongoing problems that you or the other woman are having? Where would you like some help? Where do you think you could offer it?

Back and forth between houses	Situation or problem:	
Ways that you can help the other person:		Ways you could use some help:

Discipline and consequences	Situation or problem:	
Ways that you can help the other person:		Ways you could use some help:

Responsibility and chores	Situation or problem:	
Ways that you can help the other person:		Ways you could use some help:

School and homework	Situation or problem:	
Ways that you can help the other person:		**Ways you could use some help:**

TV and computer time	Situation or problem:	
Ways that you can help the other person:		**Ways you could use some help:**

Allowance	Situation or problem:	
Ways that you can help the other person:		**Ways you could use some help:**

Playdates and friends	Situation or problem:	
Ways that you can help the other person:		**Ways you could use some help:**

Misbehavior	Situation or problem:	
Ways that you can help the other person:	Ways you could use some help:	

Meals and good health	Situation or problem:	
Ways that you can help the other person:	Ways you could use some help:	

Use this list to initiate a conversation with the other woman and ask her how you can help make her life easier. Follow the steps in Chapter Four for initiating a meeting in person and you're on your way!

RESOURCES TO EXPLORE

Books

- *Radical Collaboration: Five Essential Skills to Overcome Defensiveness and Build Successful Relationships,* by James W. Tamm and Ronald J. Luyet
- *Personal Development for Smart People: The Conscious Pursuit of Personal Growth,* by Steve Pavlina
- *Keeping Kids Out of the Middle: Child-Centered Parenting in the Midst of Conflict, Separation, and Divorce,* by Benjamin D. Garber, Ph.D.

Web sites

- The DHX: The Doughtie Houses Exchange (www.thedhx.com)
- Postcards from Splitsville (www.postcardsfromsplitsville.com/)
- Bonus Families (www.bonusfamilies.com/)

AS WE LEAVE THE CHAPTER

This is what it's like to be *down in the trenches,* re-creating your two families into something new, whole, and improved. Not "trenches" as in *warfare,* more like overhauling a formerly overgrown, scraggly garden—and turning it into something vibrant and new—working the soil, getting your hands dirty. It might feel scary and potentially volatile, but you can do it and do it *well.* Strengthen your family even more by taking a closer look at what kind of results your efforts are producing and continue to fine-tune.

6

Be Accountable

(No One Else to Blame)

STAY IN YOUR ROOM!

*It's all too easy to confuse taking responsibility for your actions with "being wrong." Remember what it was like to be little and get in trouble? You'd have given almost **anything** to squirm out from under the weight of getting caught, being **bad.** As adults, we all understand the discomfort and embarrassment of being reprimanded for a mistake at work. But being accountable for your behavior is about more than being right or wrong. It's the dark tunnel you have to go through to come out the other side into light, and change.*

A LOOK BACK FROM US

Jennifer: I had just rewritten the marketing section of the book proposal for the book you now hold in your hands, removing Carol completely from any promotional involvement, at her request. She would still actively create the content once we got a contract, but as far as talking about the book afterward, that was it—she was out.

I was beside myself with despair. Who would want this project now, without our "hook"? Carol was either in it completely, or such a phantom that she really wasn't there at all. I couldn't figure out how to frame it.

And yet, there was no denying it. I had been instrumental in Carol's decision.

What had happened?

Days before, she had explained how she had recently pulled away from being an active, hands-on stepmother. I hadn't realized the cumulative effect of all the bits and pieces she'd been telling me recently, but here was the big picture: no more disciplining the kids at all. Period.

That responsibility had been completely handed over to David (my ex, her husband).

I felt terrible, hearing her describe how she'd needed to step outside the minefield for her own sanity, to put a halt to the occasional heartbreak and the incessant stress. She'd pulled back to bring more peace to her home and marriage, but now she had a different problem—she'd landed hard in a pit of despair and powerlessness.

She had given up.

And she didn't want to feel like some liar, giving talks or interviews, nodding her head and parroting some party line she didn't believe in.

My heart was heavy as I considered how this must feel for everyone in their household. But it all came back to this: David and I had made a grievous error from the very beginning. We'd let Carol fill a vacuum created by us.

David and I are consciously aware of the fact that we're uneven disciplinarians. Embarrassing, but it's the truth, and we both know it. We mean well but are often wildly inconsistent. Over the years, we've had countless talks about parenting issues, brainstorming possible causes of conflict, creating plans for improvement. Sometimes our lofty intentions come to fruition, but oftentimes not.

Carol was organized, self-disciplined, and eager to create order and routine when she and David got together nine years ago. She'll also be the first to tell you that the situation was ripe for her own control-freak issues to kick in beautifully, an organizer walking into a messy living room in dire need of de-cluttering.

We set her up, unknowingly, David and I. We doomed her to conflict and resistance from our daughters. We put her in the intractable position of being in charge of creating change while undercurrents that maintained the status quo (that would be, uh . . . the rest of us) raged as strong as ever. We were lazy, unaware; it all seemed so wonderfully convenient.

So now there was another vacuum, one that had to be filled the *right* way. There was no getting around the hard facts: If we didn't want to jeopardize the stability of yet another family unit, David and I had to step up to the plate and make some monster course corrections, whether we knew how to or not. Time to put the power and responsibility right back where they belonged. Time to figure out how to do this, and do it right.

Carol and I talked in person in the kitchen when I picked up M. last weekend. Ironically, the issues we were all struggling with were the same sticking points that needed to go in the book. Matter of fact, we couldn't write the story without it! Things were going exactly as they needed to.

Carol brightened noticeably when we looked at things this way. Right—so she'd pulled herself out of the wind tunnel earlier, but it still wasn't working. Now David and I were stepping back in where we should have been all along. Only time would tell whether she could truly breathe a sigh of relief.

I tentatively asked her how she'd feel about returning to our original plan with the book, given the freedom to present her feelings and experiences authentically. She surprised me by reacting with genuine excitement. We thought of the masses of stepmoms and moms out there who struggled with the same issues. Cool! We could help them, too—we were just drilling down to the juicier stuff. We'd make it work . . . .

Carol: I come from a family with a lot of discipline and tough love. Soon after I met my "new" family, I realized discipline didn't play a strong part in anything, and that bugged me. I felt the girls were poorly behaved most of the time, and their mom and dad let them get away with murder.

This was mainly a problem for me when the girls were at our house, and so I came to dread our weekend visitation. I was very confused about my role as stepmother. I didn't know whether I should step into the role of disciplinarian or just stand back and let David do it his way.

I browsed some stepmother books and Web sites, trying to find a consensus about it. Some said, "Be their friend and let the parents do the hard part." Some said, "Do what seems right." Some said, "Take the mother role without stepping on 'her' toes."

So I chose to do what seemed right to me, which was to provide discipline where I saw it was seriously lacking. I thought I could make a difference—teach the girls to be better behaved and show their parents how it was done in the process. Lead by example.

The girls responded well to it, but I quickly realized one or two days a week just wasn't going to make a difference.

About two years into it, when Jennifer and I were on the road toward a good relationship, I decided to call a meeting. I had heard Jen and David complain countless times about the girls and their poor behavior, so I thought I could talk them into some changes.

We met at an "in the middle" restaurant and talked for hours. They agreed with me that changes needed to be made. They agreed that we needed a list of rules that spanned the houses. Unfortunately, they kind of balked on the idea of consequences in any more specific way than there should probably be some. I wanted a list that was kind of like "do this—this happens." But I was happy to start with the list of rules.

I typed it up and made two copies. We posted them in our houses. They were fairly vague, but it was a good start.

At our house, I constantly referred to the rules and gave time-outs where appropriate. And it really seemed to be working, though it generally took a day to remember whenever they came to our house. I quickly realized they weren't being enforced at the other house, and of course, David had no part in it, either.

Add to this the fact that the older the girls got, the more resistant they were to any discipline from me. I was frustrated.

So I called more meetings, and every time Jennifer and David said, "Okay, we'll make some changes—we're really going to do it this time." Maybe they thought things were changing, but to me it was too minimal to mean anything and I was frustrated.

After seven years, I decided to step back from the disciplinarian role. This was a two-step decision. It started with S. one year, and M. a couple years later. I fell into a kind of depression both times because I was essentially giving up, and it felt bad. Really bad.

Then came a period of understanding. I started to realize more about myself and my somewhat selfish reasons for trying to "fix" the girls. I had seen it as a challenge. That and I wanted to "show them how it was done" from a place of ego. And when my way didn't work (partly because I expected too much too fast perhaps), my pride was seriously hurt. Which could certainly account for the depression afterward.

I also came to understand Jen more, and David. They both had their own reasons for their parenting styles. We all have little (and big) traumas from our own childhoods that inform the way we parent. I had walked into a minefield and started stomping. When I took the time to look more closely, I saw things completely differently. It's a work in progress.

JOURNAL

What aspects of our stories sound familiar to you? Do you feel as if you're being made "wrong" in your relationship with the other woman?

_____

_____

_____

_____

_____

_____

_____

_____

_____

_____

_____

_____

_____

_____

_____

_____

_____

_____

_____

_____

A DEFINITION

What is accountability anyway? Basically, it's taking responsibility for the choices you've already made and the results you created—you own it, all of it. It's the willingness to see where you might have actually gone wrong and then do something about it, make amends or create redress. Put another way, you fix a problem without shifting the blame elsewhere.

To whom do I owe this courtesy?

Who are you accountable to? Do you *owe* the mother or stepmother in your life any accounting or explanation for how you act with her? Is she obligated to provide you with the same?

We would venture to say you're accountable to the people who are affected by your actions. So that would mean, yes—you're accountable to the other woman, to your children or stepchildren, to the spouse or romantic partner, and, of course, you're accountable to yourself as well.

Pie Chart: Who are you accountable to?

In this moment, right now, who do you *feel* you are accountable to when it comes to how things are going between you and the other woman? There is no right answer here. It's just a chance to rate your feelings as they are in the present. Color in the pie chart to rate your levels. We'll be coming back to this later for a closer look.

THE BENEFITS OF BEING ACCOUNTABLE

The delicate dance of trust

Accountability creates trust, a vital element in relationships. You already have experience with the different varieties. There's the taken-for-granted trust you have with people you're close to, the ones who know all your dirt. The functional, practical trust you have with coworkers. There's the underground river of trust between you and your friends; the simple, surface trust between you and acquaintances.

As the level of mutual need and dependency goes up, so does the level of risk, because both parties *need* something from each other. To a certain extent, trust involves the forming of an implicit agreement. If the agreement falls apart, both sides could end up hurt, angry, and possibly feeling taken advantage of or betrayed.

The stepmom needs to know that the mom will respect her way of doing things. That she has every right to establish rules and principles in her home, guidelines that are just as valid and important as the mom's. She needs to know that her responses and emotional reactions to the children, good or bad, are as valid as anything either bio-parent might feel—they're not secondary in importance or inferior because they're outside the insular, "original" family bubble.

The stepmom may sometimes need space from the whole chaotic jumble that is a stepfamily, since this is probably not what she imagined for herself when she envisioned a family. She wants respect. She wants closeness. She just wants to be appreciated for who she is and not treated like a permanent outsider.

And moms need to know that the stepmom will not be subtly working to undermine her, to turn the children against her. She needs to know that, while the children now have a different world to immerse themselves in, their old one is still respected and held in a certain esteem. She needs to know that if she starts bumping up against difficult behavior in her children, it's not just because she's a bad mother and the stepmom is better.

She needs to know that the stepmom is not in secret competition with her, wanting to lure the kids from their home with promises of fun and material goods that she can't provide. She wants respect. She wants closeness. She wants to be appreciated for who she is and not treated like a permanent threat.

When one or both sides first reach out to each other, to risk something of themselves and work together, it can feel pretty scary. Even if it's over something as simple as helping little Jane transport her art supplies from house to house without always losing a marker, or keeping Mark the man-child from continually sneaking out of the house and into trouble, it's more important than ever that both sides play fairly. Both sides are responsible for their mistakes or errors in judgment. If the mom tries to pull a fast one and shift the blame, the stepmom now needs to protect herself from more of the same in the future. But if the mother is honest about her agenda when she sees that her actions have caused harm, the stepmom is more likely to believe she can *relax* into the relationship and continue to build a foundation of connection and partnership.

Fixing the now

Accountability also means that mistakes are not being perpetuated. We've all experienced inane procedures at work. Everyone knows the procedures are stupid, but no one is ultimately responsible, so no one takes action. Accountability creates room for change for two reasons: You're taking ownership, and you're dealing with the truth and not trying to cover it up or hide from it. You're free to describe problems as they really are, not waste time, effort, and your integrity trying to spin the facts. You get to look at the situation starkly and decide what changes might be necessary, or even welcome.

Sometimes that initial sweeping assessment gets confused by other feelings. Let's take a closer look at this dynamic in the following quiz.

Quiz: Finger-pointing paradise

Do any of these phrases sound familiar? Mark a check by the ones you know you've heard in your head before. Fill in the blanks where necessary.

_____ *She's* the one who brings all this negativity to our relationship.

_____ It wasn't *my* idea to do things this way.

_____ Who in their *right mind* would ever _____?

_____ We'd get along a lot better *if only* she'd _____.

_____ It's not *my* fault there's no map for this kind of
impossible situation.

_____ *When* is she ever going to stop _____?

_____ *She's* the one who always forgets to _____.

_____ How is *anyone* supposed to make this work?

_____ Why should *I* be the one to do all the hard work?

_____ Why is all this crap happening to *me?*

JOURNAL

What *motifs* do you regularly return to in your thinking about the mom
or stepmom? Do you get a sense of thought patterns that might benefit
from closer inspection, in terms of taking personal responsibility?

_____

_____

_____

_____

_____

_____

_____

_____

_____

_____

_____

_____

_____

_____

_____

_____

_____

_____

_____

WHAT ACCOUNTABILITY LOOKS LIKE IN ACTION

What stands in the way

As anyone can see, blaming others gets you nowhere. So why do we do it? *Because it can feel so uncomfortable to own your mistakes.* You might feel a terrible sense of pressure and shame, even humiliation. In the moment, accountability seems to leave you even worse off than you were before. It can trigger your fears of inadequacy, of being a failure or a loser. So let's look at what it's like when you go all the way *through* those negative feelings.

Actually doing the work

It starts with self-reflection. You might begin with a vague feeling that something is not right, something is not working. You may be aware of something the other woman is doing that's "not fair," but you also have a weird feeling about yourself, too. Ask yourself if there's anything you think you should have done differently. If you could redo the experience, what would you change? What would make you feel "blameless"? How could you have acted so that you felt proud of your behavior—free and clear? Not from that old sense of competitiveness we've described in previous chapters, but simply from a place of clarity?

Pie on our face

Often, admitting mistakes we've made to ourselves begins with the phrase "*Well* . . . maybe I shouldn't have _____ after all." Or "Maybe I should have handled this situation by doing _____ instead." This is one of the bravest things you can do! You may feel completely squirmy looking your troubles squarely in the face, but don't turn back now.

How can you turn your mistakes into *action* and repair any damage you might have done? What needs to change? Is there anything you need to apologize for, independent of external factors? Are there routines between houses that need addressing? Are there changes needed in your parenting, rules, consequences, and ways of relating or communicating?

Flipping grievances over

Here's another way to approach some of those questions, if you find yourself stumped or reluctant to take on the "burden" of accountability. Turn your grievances around and ask a question:

- What can I do, *just me,* to make this situation better?
- In what way am I contributing to this problem?
- What am I *not doing* that's contributing to this problem?
- How can I better understand this person that I have a problem with?
- What is underdeveloped in me? How can I "grow" this quality or behavior?

Take another look at the Finger-Pointing Paradise Quiz you took a few pages back. Notice that many of these questions begin with Who, When, and Why—a tactic that author John G. Miller says not only subtly reinforces your own lack of culpability but also strengthens your own sense of helplessness. When you approach your "mistakes" from the perspective of the questions above, you see that accountability helps you diffuse fear, shame, and the need to hide. Your answers will energize you, empower you, and help you make better choices in the moment.

JOURNAL

Can you approach being accountable from a spirit of openness and strength? Can you leave the resentment, competitiveness, and feeling like a victim behind? Can you be open to feedback about your previous behavior and your new plan of action? What do you think?

_____

_____

_____

_____

_____

_____

_____

SOME ADDITIONAL CHALLENGES TO PRACTICING ACCOUNTABILITY

There are other tough realities that require maturity to handle. Face it: You're going to screw up. They're going to screw up. Situations are still going to go wrong, and there are *many* issues that are just outside your control. There will be miscommunications, stubbed toes, innocent mistakes that cause uncomfortable ripples. How will you handle the inevitable hiccups?

Expect personal commitments to be lopsided over time. There may be occasions when you try to take responsibility and are working hard, while she coasts. Then the positions will reverse, as you find yourself snowed under by various changes in your life. Take the long view and allow for variations in each other's efforts and commitment to change. Also, the long view will help you to not take problems personally or attribute ill intentions to the other side that may not be there.

Another issue you may grapple with is the element of vulnerability. We've talked about how scary it can be to try to create trust with the mom or stepmom, as you own your mistakes and open yourself up to scrutiny. Is there such a thing as *too much* vulnerability?

When we first became friends, we both went through times where we felt too exposed. It was awkward, thinking that your former adversary now knew some of your worst secrets and shortcomings. We both wondered in the backs of our minds if those dark shadows were going to be used against us in the future. We've also both struggled with the feeling that now, "we're supposed to be buddies—no more disagreements," which is entirely unrealistic. The way we handled it was to pull back at times, and create a little healthy distance. Once we got our bearings, we felt comfortable interacting with the other person again.

Examining your real agenda

In *Peace Is Every Step,* Vietnamese Buddhist monk Thich Nhat Hanh suggests we periodically check in with loved ones and ask them directly if they think we're doing a good job loving them. He recommends just putting it out there: Ask your loved ones if you're doing anything to hurt them, and ask them how you can do a better job.

It takes guts to ask questions like that, and hear the answers. Whether you ever ask the stepmom or mom a tamer, less gooey version of those questions, it's good to examine the answers yourself, so you can determine your real agenda.

Ask yourself, what am I trying to *get* from this other person? Am I doing a good job of treating *her* well? Could I do better?

It's worth taking the broader perspective and asking yourself, of all the people in your life: How well do I love these people? Do I love them based on what *they* seem to need and want? Or based on what *I* think they need, what I feel comfortable giving them? How much are my actions based on *getting* what I want from them in return—a secret bargain, of sorts?

How much do you altruistically give to those you love, no strings attached? In what ways are you stubbornly holding on to outdated ideas about what you feel is "appropriate" to give to others, even though they keep trying to tell you otherwise? There is much to be gained from trying to understand what other people need and want, from their perspective, *first*.

WHAT ABOUT THE MAN?

Notice what kind of energy your relationship with the husband or ex-husband puts into the stepmother/ex-wife relationship. His actions greatly influence which direction you go with the other woman, toward honesty and accountability, or toward blame and muddled facts.

If he emphasizes fairness, caution, and aims to get both sides of the story, then he's contributing to taking responsibility. If he takes solace in finger-pointing, sees either you or the both of you as victims, or gets stirred up by anger and resentment, then he contributes to blame and a continuation of the problems. Just because the wife and husband are married doesn't mean the allegiance will lie along those lines either, although that's often the norm. Sometimes it's ex and ex against the stepmom, sometimes it's husband and wife against the mother.

Another important element is communication. From whom do you get your information? Are stories consistent or constantly changing? Do you speak to each other? If the husband/ex-husband is the conduit for information, situations can easily become mangled. Messages may get relayed and changed in the telling, causing miscommunication and mis-understandings. All the more reason to work through your issues with the other woman, so you can deal with problems head-on and firsthand.

EXTRA REASSURANCE

Don't worry, we're not expecting you to bare your soul to the mom or stepmom, like baring your neck to a vampire. Take your time. Find a balance. Just be honest with yourself—that's what will really cause your perspective to shift and your feelings to lighten.

What if you feel like the other side is completely intractable? You can still make headway with your relationship, even if she doesn't change *at all.* Remember, you'll be looking at the truth of your own actions and whether they help or hinder you when it comes to creating a positive relationship with the other woman. You have the opportu-nity to make necessary changes and to feel better about what *you* bring to the table. That opportunity is independent of what the other woman is or isn't doing.

If need be, get extra support from a wise, supportive friend, someone who knows what direction you're trying to go. Talk to them honestly about where you fudged, what you'd like to do about it, and brainstorm some options.

Quiz: Where am I with accountability now?

Let's see where you are with accountability in real life. Rate your level of comfort with each statement of ability on a scale of one to five. One represents the least comfortable and five represents the most comfortable.

1 2 3 4 5 Willingness to own mistakes
1 2 3 4 5 Willingness to get feedback about how to
              proceed
1 2 3 4 5 Willingness to make amends and apologize

1 2 3 4 5   Willingness to feel the discomfort of being "wrong"

1 2 3 4 5   Willingness to ask questions from a new angle

1 2 3 4 5   Willingness to make different choices in the moment

1 2 3 4 5   Willingness to see how *I* can help make things better

Scoring Guide

If you scored mostly ones, whoa, we're surprised you made it to the end of the chapter!

If you scored mostly twos, you're starting to see some glimmering possibilities.

If you scored mostly threes, you may still associate being accountable with "getting in trouble," but you're getting there.

If you scored mostly fours, you're stepping up and doing well.

If you scored mostly fives, you are an evolved being and may well be from outer space.

JOURNAL

How'd you do? What areas were most comfortable for you? Which ones felt like walking on burning coals?

_____

_____

_____

_____

_____

_____

_____

_____

_____

_____

_____

_____

RESOURCES TO EXPLORE

Books

- *QBQ! The Question Behind the Question: Practicing Personal Accountability in Work and in Life,* by John G. Miller
- *The Four Agreements: A Practical Guide to Personal Freedom, A Toltec Wisdom Book,* by Don Miguel Ruiz
- *The Miracle of Mindfulness,* by Thich Nhat Hanh

Web sites

- Personal Growth Planet (www.personalgrowthplanet.com/)
- Zen Habits (www.zenhabits.net/)
- The Change Blog (www.thechangeblog.com/)

AS WE LEAVE THE CHAPTER

Being *wrong* never felt so good, did it? On the outside, taking responsibility may look like it's the last thing you want to do, but it's the one step you might be most proud of taking. Taking absolute and complete responsibility for your actions is ultimately a powerful, freeing way to live. And it can work miracles in your relationship with the mom or stepmom in your life.

What's something simple you do every day that is a huge contributor to the inadvertent mistakes you make with the other woman? Read on for a closer look at communication.

7

Communicate

(Or, Why Aren't You a Mind Reader?)

ON THE ONE HAND . . .

You always have a choice to make when it comes to communication: You can communicate to foster harmony between you and the step-mother or ex-wife in your life, or you can communicate to try to gain the upper hand. You can listen only halfheartedly, or listen from a place of openness and neutrality. You can take comfort in repeating familiar complaints and criticism, or you can channel your frustrations into productive actions. The choice is yours.

A LOOK BACK FROM US

Carol: I remember the time David was talking to Jennifer on the phone about letting the girls live with us. I remember her calling frequently to complain that the girls were totally out of hand and she couldn't control them. I felt like that was a pretty good reason to have them come live with us, so they could have two parents instead of one, since I could stay home with them. And to be honest, I did feel like I could provide better structure and discipline. The fact is that I'm not perfect and I've since realized, with the girls and J. too, that parenting is much harder than it looks. But at that time, I thought I could do it *better.*

And I remember talking to Jennifer on the phone during that call and saying, "We'll take them off your hands," or something like that, and her saying, "*What* are you talking about? I want to keep them!" She wasn't mean or anything, but I guess I had misunderstood. I thought that perhaps she was at the end of her rope, and was just ready for us to have them. Not for good, not as in giving them away, but just switching the custody, so that we were the primaries and she got visits. But that wasn't the case at all and after Jennifer said that, I got off the phone and went into the shower and sat there, bawling, for a good long time.

And after that, I tried to just forget it had happened. Feelings were so volatile back then . . . .

Another time Jennifer called in tears saying she simply had to get a full-time job and couldn't do it with the girls getting home early after school and she was ready for them to live with us. At least, that's what David relayed to me. So we came and picked them up, along with all their stuff. And we bought another car, so I could have one in case of an emergency. They lived with us for about a month and then one day she came to pick them up and said, "Okay, I'm ready for them to come back." That really got me.

Jennifer: I don't remember things as specifically as Carol does, but I do know that the situation between us at the time was pretty horrible. I tried to avoid talking to Carol as much as possible, whether on the phone or in person. When we did speak, our conversations were often subtly argumentative or just plain confusing. I tried to just go through David for important details, but it wasn't always easy to talk to him, either. I was jealous of the fact that Carol was at home and I was struggling to make it on part-time work (initially), since I didn't want the girls having to stay at school even longer in after-school care. I felt like I just couldn't win—I was either broke and home with them, or facing parental neglect, guilt, and a higher income.

I was also really struggling as a single parent. I know the girls had to grapple with their own difficult feelings about the divorce (which I won't go into here), and I think we were all often on edge. When things would reach a feverish pitch, sometimes I would call David to either vent, get help, or somehow make him wrong. Not a pretty picture any way you look at it, but one that is, I'm sure, fairly common.

I don't remember the sequence either for how the girls ended up going over to their house for a short period. I do know that the way it seemed at the time was that I wanted David (and, implicitly, Carol, but mostly David) to be more involved in parenting and to have to shoulder more of the responsibility. Things seemed lopsided and unfair to me back then. I do remember one conversation very vividly, where David suggested that the girls would be better off living with them, since Carol "was at home and could be with them" and I was always "so stressed out about work." I went ballistic at that, him assuming a "perfect stranger" (sorry, Carol) could do a better job than I could at raising my own children! He's since apologized profusely for the comment, and it's all water under the bridge.

I'm sure David and I discussed things on the phone and didn't come to any clear point of agreement, because our resentments usually got in the way of clarity. Nevertheless, the girls went to live at their house for what I assumed was going to be a few weeks, so I could gather my wits about me and recalibrate. I missed them desperately and when I went to go pick them up, I don't remember any problems with that.

It sure did seem like when it came to discussions and plans and agreements, there were always misunderstandings, or flat-out different interpretations of the same event. Honestly, I look back at that time as being pretty stomach-churning.

JOURNAL

So what about you? Which way do you want things to go with the other woman? Do you want to work toward cooperation, peace, and harmony? Or would you rather just shoot for the path of least resistance? Can you relate to the stress and confusion of our stories?

_____

_____

_____

_____

_____

_____

_____

_____

_____

_____

_____

_____

_____

_____

_____

_____

_____

_____

_____

_____

COMMUNICATION 101

Brushing up

You'd think all this communication business would be easy—after all, think of how many thoughts and sentences you say and hear every day—but it's such an important function that it still bears careful analysis. We're so used to our own communication patterns that we don't usually give our habits, or the results they create, much conscious consideration. How can you convey information, resolve problems, and create cooperation more effectively? Communicating well is a skill that can be mastered—if you're willing to go back and reexamine the basics. Let's start with the two main components, listening and expressing yourself, then we'll take a look at a simple formula you can fall back on to make your intentions clearer. Finally, we'll talk a bit about basic manners.

Can you hear me now?

When you listen to the other woman, are you really *listening?* Or like us in the descriptions above, are you at the mercy of an underlying static that makes it hard to understand others and absorb information and intentions? Do you constantly counter the speaker in your mind, keeping up a private argument with her? If someone were to ask you *after the fact,* how accurately would you be able to recount the other person's concerns, needs, and fears?

The next time you're in a conversation with the stepmom or mom, try a little game. See if you can circumvent the traditional one-up/one-down dynamic where each side is attempting to control the conversation and push it toward her own agenda. Experiment with making yourself "under" her, or submissive to her, instead of "over" her. Clarify a simple point you'd like to make for yourself first, and then metaphorically step aside when you feel her trying to engage your argumentative side. It doesn't mean you're giving up and it doesn't mean she's going to "win," either; it's just another way to be in a conversation. Soften yourself and aim for a calm feeling of equality between you. See what happens!

Listening to someone really well and truly understanding her needs is the only way to get her to do the same with *you*.

Identify your target

When it comes to expressing yourself more clearly, you have to first determine your goal or intent. Would you like to get the other person's help with a problem you are having? Is some behavior of *hers* the problem? Are you looking for more brainpower for some open-ended problem-solving? Are you simply seeking sympathy, commiseration, and understanding? Get clear on your goal before you engage in a counterproductive discussion that might take you even further away from where you're trying to go.

The awesome transformative powers of "thank you" and "hello"

They're a social lubricant, a path through the thorny woods, an accepted mechanism for interaction in the world of people, sometimes very obnoxious people. Manners. Remember those? No matter where you are on the spectrum of ex-wife/stepmother relationships, you can't go wrong if you use them.

Let's say you're stuck with an annoying relative at the family reunion, or your creepy boss at the office party. In those instances, you'd have to buck up, play nice, and grit your teeth and bear it—unless you wanted to potentially jeopardize your job or become the next unwitting victim of a familial gossip campaign.

So you'd lean on your manners, and maybe lean hard. You'd put in the effort required to nod your head while the other person droned on and on, got too close to your face with spiked-punch- or potato-salad breath, or asked inappropriate questions about when you were going to have your first/another kid. You'd say *umm-hmm* and smile here and there, even if it was plastered onto your face like spackling. Maybe you'd ask a follow-up question to show you were listening, all the while looking for a way to make your getaway.

It's not *bad* that you're looking for an escape—after all, you're not obligated to want to be Aunt Edna's or Creepy Earl's best friend just because they're talking to you, but still, you'd do the right thing, put in your time, restrain the impulse to bolt from the room or picnic table with your arms flailing, and when it seemed right, you'd flag someone else down or excuse yourself to go to the bathroom.

You'd think of something.

Well, that same little dance of tolerance is what's required with the mother or stepmother in your life, at first, if you ever want to get along with her. We're not actually asking you to dip down inside yourself and discover a veritable well of warm and fuzzy feelings if the warm feelings just aren't there. What we *are* asking you to do is go through the rituals, even if you'd rather she lived on an island all alone, far, far away, perhaps with just one coconut tree and very little in the way of shelter.

We're asking you to greet her with the little pleasantries and fillers we all use to talk to people we don't know or necessarily want to spend time with (like the cashier at the store, a coworker with habits that grate on your nerves, or an overbearing neighbor)—to think ahead a little bit, to be considerate.

Think about this: What happens when a cashier at a store is deliberately rude to you? If you're like most people, immediately all your defenses go up and, based on your personality, you react (crumble, strike back, go over their heads to complain, do something passive-aggressive, etc.). *You* instinctively know when you're not being treated with just the "normal," requisite amount of good manners. The ex-wife or stepmother in your life picks up on the same thing.

But what happens when that same cashier is at least saying "please" and "thank you" and "have a nice day" to you, along with the gruff manner and lack of eye contact? If you can see that the cashier is making that rudimentary effort, suddenly it's so much easier to depersonalize the negative behavior: maybe the cashier is just having a bad day, or hates the job, or has family problems.

Suddenly, you feel compassion for them. You see them as a real person, someone who's struggling to keep their head above water just like anyone else—just like you. And so you magnanimously offer a smile or reassuring word, and put some extra warmth into your own wishes for a nice day.

This is what manners do: They let the other person know that he or she is valued simply as a human being. Manners equalize, make bad behavior less about you, and help others empathize.

Lean on your manners with the other woman, even when you don't want to. Perhaps especially when you don't want to! On a subtle level, you'll be signaling a softening up on your part to the other person, an intention to respect and connect. Some part of her subconscious will perk up and pay attention, as in, *Hmmm, something's different here. I don't detect so much "enemy energy." What's going on?*

That heightened attention is a very good thing. It can pave the way to openness on her part and next thing you know, you might find yourselves creating one small moment of meeting each other halfway, even if it's something as simple as a quick smile or a genuine "hello."

CONSEQUENCES OF POOR COMMUNICATION

Communicating poorly has real consequences. We often use our conversations, without thinking, to bolster our position and display knowledge and superiority. What is poor communication? In the context of this book, it means you:

- Forget to mention important, relevant facts and details.
- Change plans and don't update the other person.
- Don't emphasize the necessary information to make sure that you're being understood.
- Consistently fall into the sinkhole of blame and get sidetracked—and fail to communicate completely.

- Are deliberately obscure in an attempt to set the other person up to fail.
- Don't communicate at all and try to shift the burden for action to the other side/person.
- Use cold, unwelcoming body language, such as crossed arms, lack of eye contact, and a set jaw in response to the other person.

JOURNAL

Does any of that sound familiar? How so? Are you often on the receiving end of this behavior or the giving end?

_____

_____

_____

_____

_____

_____

_____

_____

_____

_____

_____

A bad game of "telephone"

Poor communication creates conflict and confusion. Did you ever play "telephone" when you were little? Everyone sits in a circle and someone begins by whispering a sentence or phrase into his or her neighbor's ear. That person in turn whispers the same phrase to his or her neighbor until finally the game ends where it began. When the last and first person announce what the secret was supposed to be, their two versions are usually completely different. Poor communication creates the same problem—you may think you're all moving forward on the same page, only to find out that you're at odds with each other when you hit a wall and end up disagreeing about what happened.

There's also the passive/aggressive "forgetting" or withholding of information, a very common occurrence between divorced families and stepfamilies. While it's sometimes easy to simply forget to mention an important detail, such as a change in pickup time for the kids or a change of date for the school conference, this "oops" can also be done deliberately. Such tactics undermine trust in the relationship and increase blame and further complications.

The lesser of two evils

Mangled information also leads to bad decisions. If you don't have all the facts, you can't accurately weigh the potential risks and benefits when you're at a fork in the road. If you press forward anyway, you'll often back yourself into a corner, having to choose between two unattractive options. Problems remain or actually get worse. You're also hampered when it comes to getting closer to your ultimate goal, because you're still not clearly seeing the parameters of the situation. You don't feel supported or understood either.

The guilt of gossip

Gossip always comes back to bite you in the ass. And with stepmothers and ex-wives in particular, there seems to be plenty of it to go around. Think about it: The setup is perfect. You're probably privy to the odd personal detail about each other, and yet, if you're like most women in this situation, you've also got plenty of safe, isolating distance between you as you give each other a w-i-d-e berth out of dislike and distaste. The other woman may have quirky social phobias, compulsively spend large amounts of money that she can't afford on _____ (fill in the blank), or have outlandish and wildly ambitious dreams about someday doing/being/seeing _____ (fill in the blank again with something ridiculous). Whatever her dirty little secrets or outrageous acts of stupidity and incompetence, if you two aren't getting along, those factoids are the perfect fodder for that most human of pastimes—clucking away about the most inane prattle, dabbling in defamation, basking in belittlement.

Despite the thrill of spite, gossiping is a potentially dangerous prospect—akin to lying—with a lot at stake. Of course, this is usually only obvious in hindsight, when you're kicking yourself, so maybe it's a good thing to think about *beforehand*. There's secrecy, ill will, a sprinkling of deceit. And then there are the logistics of keeping versions of reality straight. This usually takes some deliberate effort and forethought, creating a nice little undercurrent of fear and anxiety so all your gossip stays covered up and properly secured.

But if your earful ever makes it to *her* ears, watch out! This can easily become the stuff of war. You may be up shit creek for a good, long while.

Then . . . you're even worse off.

THINKING BACKWARD

Although it's no fun, ask yourself—what damage might result from your gossip being discovered? What trust do you stand to lose (and not just hers, either)? What credibility will you now have to work to regain? What consequences might you now have to face?

Yep, gossiping usually creates guilt and shame. You know it's wrong (and yet . . . ahhh, the temptation). How do you know this? While you may still feel "justified" if the other person's actions suck, there's still a part of you that holds basic standards for the way you should treat people in the back of your mind. And the ultimate litmus test: Would you want someone *else* to be talking this way about *you?* Probably not, but the lure is so strong because of the payoffs.

We gossip to feel superior to others; to vent frustration and a feeling of powerlessness; to generate sympathy from listeners while we regale with tales of victimization or audacious nerve—even to indulge that dark part of ourselves that is really and truly delighting in the misery and struggles of another. But just like a drinking spree that feels momentarily freeing and crazy, you'll pay for it afterward when your natural sense of human decency kicks back in.

EXTERNAL REALITIES

Maybe the worst consequence is how your life actually works out there in the world. When you gossip, you're saying things about someone that you would never say to his or her face. Not that you should always say *everything you think* to someone directly, but in this case, there's probably a huge gap between your thoughts and actions. Do you say a bright, tight hello and shoot the stepmom or mom visual darts dipped in poison? Do you pretend to be cooperative on the phone, but look for reasons why her plans or requests "just won't work for us"? Do you roll your eyes in her presence when her back is turned? Act nice, but then bitch about her to the kids?

Since you're hiding something when you hang someone's dirty laundry out to dry in your own backyard, you've got to keep an eye on what's out there in the public domain of interaction, just like a lie. This creates a certain kind of brittleness and superficiality in your behavior. It feels gross and uncomfortable to you, and it probably feels weird to the other person too, whether you realize it or not. Plus, feeling guilty just makes you want to get the hell away from that person (aside from whatever problems you're *also* having with her), and that's not going to help either.

The worst part about all of that is that it definitely makes it harder to connect and have something new happen between you. The guilt, the awkwardness, the avoidance—the whole dynamic keeps you frozen in conflict. Not only does it feel awful, but it's sad too, if you think about the opportunities lost.

RIPPLES IN A MURKY POND

You're in risky territory ethically, too, when you partake of gossip and secrets. If you're the one telling the secrets, the other person is going to be upset if she finds out that you've blabbed. It can be *oh so easy* to cross a line when we're emotionally "processing" and venting. Somehow, we just get caught up in our emotions and next thing you know, the snake is out of the cage and is now hiding under the couch.

Sure, it might be to your advantage to reveal what you know, but consider why you're doing it first and ask yourself: Is this worth the potential consequences? Those might be, in part, a lack of trust from all sides, including the person who first confided in you; a loss of credibility; increased distance from all parties involved; a lack of willingness to solve problems with you in the future; and the knowledge that you're not to be trusted with sensitive information.

If you're the lucky recipient of secrets and gossip, your hands are tied here, too. You're not supposed to know what you know, so that means you can't "act" on that information. And if you can't act on the truth, your complicity only perpetuates the situation. The problems remain the same, unless you're going to betray the person who revealed the secret too. You can always claim a certain innocence about your position, but you are also responsible for the fact that you didn't ask the person to stop, either. Being privy to secrets may lead you to feel guilty and keep yourself somewhat removed from others.

WHAT ABOUT THE MAN?

There's a huge potential for lopsided information flow between divorced families and stepfamilies. There may be details that are handled only by the husband and his ex-wife, such as transactions that involve money or legal issues, such as custodial arrangements. Poor communication can have major financial consequences here, too—if you can't talk disagreements through, you might end up resolving the issue in court, an even more expensive proposition. Use a group spreadsheet to keep track of records, or if there's enough trust, create a community bank account.

Stepmoms, the husband can help here in numerous ways. First, let him know you're not going to be trashing his name with the other woman (okay, maybe a little bit, out of love, but he doesn't have to know that). He could potentially provide childcare during coffee dates. He could help you stop venting about the ex-wife, if you ask him. Let him know that your family business is just that; it belongs to *both of you*. Ask him to not go around and around in negative conversational loops about the other woman anymore. Ask him to help you reframe the problems that still exist *between all of you*.

For mothers, there's a lot you can do to let him know you only have the best of intentions. Can you set aside some of your current and old grievances and focus on creating a sense of collaboration? Let your ex know that this is something that people are actually doing these days! Tell him you'd like to turn over a new leaf and invite him to join you.

For both moms and stepmoms, do your best to refrain from trash talk and psychological dissections with him and *about* him. Continue to process old baggage in the healthiest of ways and keep your inner house clean. Reiterate the positive aspects and potential benefits of you two getting along to gain his support and reinforce any changes in routines with the kids.

HARNESSING GOOD COMMUNICATION TO INCREASE TWO-FAMILY HARMONY

Keep your tools nice and shiny

Think of communication as an important tool for cooperation and harmony, capable of creating understanding, support, new ideas and solutions, and even closeness, lightness, and joy. Use it carefully and consciously. If you really want to be a pioneer, be open and forthcoming with the information that flows back and forth between households. Establish a routine of keeping facts moving cleanly and predictably between you, the other woman, and the father, and you'll head off a lot of potential problems.

Metamorphosis

So many shots of criticism are fired across the bow in mother/stepmother relationships. Why don't more women take the time to reframe their complaints into solid requests that can be acted upon? For starters, it's scary to put yourself out there—you might be rejected, ridiculed, or lose face. Somehow it just seems easier to remain disgruntled than to do the work of figuring out a reasonable outcome to ask for.

We've already covered some guidelines to keep in mind in earlier chapters, such as how to apologize, how to ask for a truce, and how to show someone you're listening during a dialogue. What follows is a simple formula to help you make your conversations clearer.

Author Dennis Rivers (*The Seven Challenges Workbook: Cooperative Communication Skills for Success at Home and at Work*) advocates using "the five I-messages" to get your point across and articulate your desires. You start by saying

1. What you observe,
2. What you're feeling,
3. Because you interpret, evaluate, or need _____.
4. You now want to request_____ and
5. You envision or hope for _____ from your request.

Seem unwieldy? Here's an example:

"I noticed that (1) Timmy has forgotten to bring his baseball uniform to practice the last couple of weeks and (2) I've been worried that he's going to have to sit out too many games (3) because he's just not organized enough to pack all the right things by himself. (4) Would you mind helping him go over his bag before you guys leave the house? (5) Maybe this will help him eventually get into the habit of packing up correctly."

When you add qualifiers or explanations to your request (as in number 3, you engage people's interest and willingness to problem-solve and to generate additional ideas you might not have thought of. In asking for help, you're also implicitly making the other person your equal, instead of commanding her, and showing the other person you respect her opinions and ideas.

EXERCISE
Now it's your turn. What's one simple problem you have with the other woman? How would you use this formula to create a sentence asking for what you want?

_____

_____

_____

_____

_____

_____

_____

FAMILY MEETINGS

Getting both families together is a great way to tackle some tough problems together and get everyone on the same page. But be careful! When you begin, make sure to start with only a few simple subjects at a time, or you'll get bogged down in overwhelming emotions and potential arguments. Try to make the experience positive in some way, like going out for dinner or dessert, or out to a park. We've said it before: Don't assault the kids all at once with a list of complaints. See if you can get them to help you brainstorm. Approach problems from the spirit of "How can we figure out these things *together* so they work better for *everyone?*" And don't be afraid to table certain difficult topics until later—this is not the only family meeting you're ever going to have! Take it slowly, build up your confidence as a larger family unit, and handle one big subject at a time.

Make sure not to leave anyone out

Even if it's inconvenient, do your best to keep everyone in the loop. Keep talking and meeting, keep up with status checks between the two houses. Communicate by e-mail and phone and meet in person on a regular basis, if possible. Staying on top of daily and weekly details increases everyone's sense of caring and involvement—a huge bonus for the kids. Some additional ideas to encourage regular, consistent communication:

- Two-minute calls/e-mail/create a Yahoo group to keep everyone in the loop
- Google docs for financial spreadsheets or notes
- Basecamp.com for big family projects that require schedules and shared documents
- Shared Google calendars (we're big fans of Google)

Regular pats on the back

Express appreciation often and catch people "doing good" whenever possible. Look at your own ratio for communication: How much of what you're saying is negative? How much is neutral? How much is positive? Many studies have shown that employees thrive with genuine, positive feedback, and yet they also say it's sadly lacking in most work environments. Family life is similar, but it doesn't have to be. Work hard to validate and acknowledge.

Do you feel awkward expressing appreciation and gratitude toward those you love (and even those you barely tolerate)? Would you be willing to up your daily quotient to see what happens? More about strengthening gratitude in Chapter Ten.

EXTRA REASSURANCE

More help for going it alone

What if one person is extremely disorganized? What if the other side is actively working to undermine your relationship by sabotaging you and your family? Here's what our kids suggested:

- Put yourself in the other person's position and see if you can understand her better. If she keeps doing it, actually ask her why she's trying to undermine you and see what she says.
- Try to turn the negative energy into something good, even if your efforts don't involve the other person. See if you can look at it from a different perspective.
- Even if it's not going swimmingly, if you're genuinely trying, then you're modeling something great for the kids.

Quiz: My communication style

Where are you with the following elements of good communication? What's your style and how well does this usually work for you? What would you like to experiment with or improve? With whom?

Listening well and increasing understanding	Overall progress:	1	2	3	4	5	6	7	8	9	10
Experiment with:					In what situation:						

Refraining from gossip and secrets	Overall progress: 1 2 3 4 5 6 7 8 9 10		
Experiment with:		In what situation:	

Using good manners	Overall progress: 1 2 3 4 5 6 7 8 9 10		
Experiment with:		In what situation:	

Turning complaints into requests	Overall progress: 1 2 3 4 5 6 7 8 9 10		
Experiment with:		In what situation:	

Family meetings and including everyone	Overall progress: 1 2 3 4 5 6 7 8 9 10		
Experiment with:		In what situation:	

Showing appreciation	Overall progress:	1	2	3	4	5	6	7	8	9	10
Experiment with:		In what situation:									

Just like with other inventories you've already taken in this book, a part of your brain is paying attention and taking note of your entries. Trust yourself to make the changes you need to make!

JOURNAL

Which elements of communication do you feel the most comfortable with? Which ones need some work? Are you looking forward to experimenting with different types of communication?

_____

_____

_____

_____

_____

_____

_____

_____

_____

_____

_____

_____

_____

_____

_____

_____

_____

RESOURCES TO EXPLORE

Books
- *Difficult Conversations: How to Discuss What Matters Most,* by Douglas Stone, Bruce Patton, and Sheila Heen
- *Nonviolent Communication: A Language of Life,* by Marshall B. Rosenberg
- *Crucial Conversations: Tools for Talking When Stakes are High,* by Kerry Patterson, Joseph Grenny, Ron McMillan, and Al Switzler

Web sites
- Divorcing Daze (www.divorcingdaze.libsyn.com/)
- Stepfamily Letter Project (www.stepfamilyletterproject.word press.com)
- New Conversations (www.newconversations.net/)

AS WE LEAVE THE CHAPTER

When you enroll the other person in your efforts to create a positive outcome to your problems by speaking to her differently, you actually convey something to her more than just your words. You signal her that you care about her input, you value her perspective, and you're open to her contributions. When you turn your focus toward future progress, you're freer to leave the past behind and create something brand-new. There may still be times when you could use a breather, though, and that's where we're heading in our next chapter.

8

Regroup

(Dust Off Your Pants When You Fall Down)

A PILE OF FIRE EXTINGUISHERS

Life is stressful, but as we've already seen, mother/stepmother relationships have some unique stressors that can really be tough to manage. Have you ever just gotten to a point with the other woman where you're about to tear your hair out? Or you feel like you're melting into a hopeless little puddle? Or like you're going to catch the curtains on fire through the sheer power of your anger alone?

In this chapter, we'll be asking you once again to turn your focus back to yourself, but this time with a different goal: to increase your ability to put yourself back together during and after a big blowout.

A LOOK BACK FROM US

Carol: Stepparenting is the toughest thing I've ever done. There have been countless times when I've wanted to kill "her," the kids, *and* my husband! But because prison doesn't appeal to me, I have refrained.

There are a few tricks I've used to remain sane. Keep in mind, this is from the stepmother's perspective, which is most often with the idea of self-preservation in mind.

1. The first might seem a little strange. It seems funny to me now, but it really helped during the early years. I used to think of Jen as two different people. There was the Jen I saw in person who was nice and intelligent and I could have a good laugh (or cry) with. Then there was the Jen I heard stories about from David, who was late picking the girls up, and who didn't uphold her end of our "across the house rule system." Thinking of her as two people really helped me be nice to the Jennifer I saw in person. Slowly, over the years, I have combined those

two people into almost one, as I came to understand her more deeply and find out where she's coming from.

2. Another good trick for me has been small escapes. There were lots of times the girls came over for the weekend and I would get so roiled up over the messes they left around the house. I would ask them to clean it up; they would smart off to me; I would get angry and yell; David would tell me I was being too harsh (in front of them); I would explode. During those times, it worked best for me to just leave the house. See a movie. Go to the mall. Preferably something that took my mind off it all so I could come back to the house calmed down, with a fresh attitude.

3. When I have been in the thick of battle with Jen or David, with us all trying to figure out why none of it's MY fault and somehow all on the other two, it has helped me to mentally stop and try to listen to them and hear where they're coming from. This is the hardest "trick" and not really a trick at all. More like work. It's something that any book about relationships will tell you. It's like exercise. We all know we should do it, but it's *hard*. Still practicing this one, but I've gotten much better.

4. Last but not least, and remember this is the stepmother talking, is the position I finally took with all this, which was abdicating responsibility to the "real" parents. Stepping back and giving up the position of disciplinarian. After eight years of stepparenting, I went to a therapist. I spent an hour telling her all about how hard I'd been trying to homeschool the youngest and how frustrating it was not getting the cooperation I wanted out of her or her parents. She said, "Why are you doing this, she's not your responsibility?!" I said "But-but-but—" then I realized she was right. These kids don't need a second mother. And if I don't agree with how Jen and David raise their kids . . . well, the hard truth is, it's not my problem. This may sound harsh, but I needed to put the burden of responsibility back where it belonged—on their shoulders.

Jennifer: Normally, we're all the Cleavers over here, so imagine my surprise when our lovely, recent, two-family Sunday brunch turned into a spontaneous group therapy session. As is often the way of family talky-talk meetings, one problem was thrown onto the pile only to be immediately smothered by another, and another, and next thing you know, someone's off in one room crying while another person is welling up in the living room, and everyone else is just sitting there, looking dazed and confused, wondering how to put things right and having not the slightest clue how to do so. (Now that's what's called a run-on!)

As a large extended family, we seem to do this upon occasion.

We'll be coasting along, and then a few issues will start building up and then, *blam*. Troubles bubble up to be addressed, or else . . . they get worse. Luckily, we've gone through this process enough times now that I think we all know on some core level that everything will all be okay. It may take awhile, but we *do* get there.

Some things that helped us that day:

1. Try to focus on one issue at a time. When we managed to do this, eventually, we could talk a problem through to a natural conclusion and then, feeling complete, we moved on.

2. Keep breathing! Even when it seems like all hell has broken loose, if you just do your best to keep the air moving through your lungs, you don't get as stirred up, and you can focus on finding a solution, or at least, on brainstorming together.

3. Listen. There seemed to be a fair amount of listening going on at our last powwow—which is maybe why the venting happened—and it can seem undesirable, at least in the short term. But in the long run, things feel *clearer*, so I guess the momentary angst is worth it. (Right? Right!)

4. If you see someone quietly struggling, say something. Doing this led to some surprising confessions that day that created even more room to get somewhere.

5. Do your best to reconnect at the end. To see us at the end of the morning, you'd never have known only nine hours earlier, we were all teetering on the edge of the cliff (kidding, it was more like an hour). By the time David, Carol, and baby walked out the front door, there was lots of laughing and hugs and thank-yous, and we were all ready for lunch.

JOURNAL

So how do you put yourself back together after conflict? During conflict? Do you have any secret tricks? Any hardy strategies that consistently generate peace, clarity, or relief?

_____

_____

_____

_____

_____

_____

_____

_____

_____

_____

HOW MANY KINDS OF CONFLICT?
LET ME COUNT THE WAYS . . .

Are you sick of hearing about how the ex-wife or stepmother "always lets us do it this way at _her_ house" when it comes to TV, the computer or video games, staying up late, chores, homework, or junk food? Perhaps the other side is stonewalling you and won't cooperate or give you necessary information, or she's continually blaming you for something that's outside your control. Maybe there's perpetual gossiping, spilling of secrets, or the telling of lies. Being ignored or shunned can be very stressful, too.

Sometimes, no matter how hard you're trying—no matter how much you're biting your tongue, trying to practice patience, forgiveness, the extreme discipline involved in failing to murder the other woman—things are still . . . bad, and you just want to give up.

From discouragement to relief

It's no surprise that we're often "triggered" in these relationships—they stir up such primitive feelings. Expect to be activated!

What's your threshold of stress? We all try to manage, up to a certain point, and then past that, we often get overwhelmed and shut down. Your limits fluctuate, depending upon what else is going on with your life. Let's see if we can raise the cap of your threshold in the healthiest possible way.

First, consider: Is there a correlation between stress relief and how well you might end up getting along with the ex-wife or stepmom that you're "stuck" with? Absolutely. Even if nothing else changes and she stays as impossible as she is at this very moment, things are already better because *you* are.

We'll approach de-stressing from both an emotional and physical perspective, and we'll further break suggestions down by what you can do *in the moment,* and what you can do *after the fact.*

HELP FOR IN THE MOMENT

What can you do in the heat of the moment? Plenty! There's not much to remember with the following tips and that's a good thing, because what happens when your stress level starts amping up? It's harder to really *hear* people, it's harder to think clearly, and your memory often starts leaking, too.

I . . . can't . . . breathe!

We've talked about the value of taking a deep breath before in this book, but not all deep breaths are created equal. As a matter of fact, if you try to take the *wrong* kind of deep breath when you're really stressed out, it's liable to make you feel even *more* anxious! Often when someone tells us to take a deep breath, we only inhale about halfway, and then when we exhale, it's in short little puffs.

Try this: breathe all the way into your diaphragm for three to five seconds. Let your belly fill up first, then your lungs. It shouldn't feel "hard" or super-tight—see if you can bring air in deliberately but gently. Hold the breath in for about two seconds, then slowly and gently exhale. Try to make the exhale last much longer than the inhale, because the exhalation is the part that will actually calm you. Shoot for about eight seconds breathing out. Again, don't force things. If you find yourself getting light-headed, you may be trying too hard.

Most of us breathe from the top of our chest only. Why? Our theory, for women at least, comes down, in part, to feeling self-conscious about our tummies. Look down at your own stomach now. Is there a slight bit of tension accumulated there? What does your stomach look like if you completely let it out? Do you accept this part of your body if it pooches out (even more)? It makes a difference!

The next stressful phone call or interaction you have with the other woman, notice whether you've started breathing quickly from your upper chest. Relax your tummy; pull nice, fresh air all the way in; let the tension go out of your body with your breath and watch your stress level start to drop.

Make the INNER voices louder

No, we're not advocating the creation of scary clown movies in your own noggin, but we *are* asking you to *listen* to what you're saying to yourself on a regular basis. Most of the time, we don't separate ourselves from the voice in our head that keeps up a constant stream of chatter, commenting on everything we see, do, say, or experience. (If we knew someone who talked this much in real life, we'd either move across town to avoid them or we'd look into industrial-strength earplugs for their visits!) But therein lies the problem: The chatter just passes on by like a stream of cars on a highway, and we don't stop to consider whether our repetitive loops of thoughts are actually helping us or hurting us.

If you stop right now, place this book in your lap, and look around the room, what do you say to yourself about what you see? What do you say about what you just read? About us as authors? About various objects in the room? About what you should be doing with your time instead of reading?

Our thoughts pass by so quickly that it's almost like they're little flashes of lightning beneath the bubble of our consciousness. But those thoughts also create an instant emotion—and our actions are typically motivated by our emotions—so it's worth slowing down and catching up to your inner monologue.

If you had an earpiece in your ear with someone constantly whispering instructions, impressions, and commentary, wouldn't you want to turn up the volume so you could know just what sort of input was being delivered to your precious brain?

The next time you find yourself in battle with the mom or step-mom, eavesdrop on yourself. Ask yourself these questions:

- What are you saying to yourself about her?
- Is this helping you move toward progress or conflict?
- What are you saying to yourself about you/about what's going to happen next/about how things *should* be?
- Can you purposefully shift your thoughts to a more positive track?

JOURNAL

What are some persistent thoughts you're well aware of regarding the other woman? What's your running commentary about your own actions? What is your inner voice predicting is going to happen between you two? (We'll get into what to do with this information later in this chapter. For now, take two minutes and jot down a few thoughts.)

_____

_____

_____

_____

_____

_____

_____

_____

_____

_____

_____

_____

_____

_____

_____

Ten Zen Seconds

Eric Maisel wrote a little gem of a book on centering techniques that take only a few seconds to implement called *Ten Zen Seconds.* He was kind enough to grant us an interview.

NOTB: What is *Ten Zen Seconds* all about? Can you give us an overview?

EM: It's actually a very simple but powerful technique for reducing your stress, getting yourself centered, and reminding yourself about how you want to live your life. It's built on the single idea of "dropping a useful thought into a deep breath."

You use a deep breath, five seconds on the inhale and five seconds on the exhale, as a container for important thoughts that aim you in the right direction in life, and you employ this breathing-and-thinking technique as the primary way to keep yourself on track.

Here are the twelve incantations or affirmations. The parentheses show how the phrase gets "divided up" between the inhale and the exhale. You inhale on the first parentheses and exhale on the second:

1. (I am completely) (stopping)
2. (I expect) (nothing)
3. (I am) (doing my work)
4. (I trust) (my resources)
5. (I feel) (supported)
6. (I embrace) (this moment)
7. (I am free) (of the past)
8. (I make) (my meaning)
9. (I am open) (to joy)
10. (I am equal) (to this challenge)
11. (I am) (taking action)
12. (I return) (with strength)

(Two small notes: The third incantation functions differently from the other eleven, in that you name something specific each time you use it, for example, "I am emptying the dishwasher" or "I am paying the bills." This helps you bring mindful awareness to each of your activities throughout the day. The eighth incantation reminds you that it is *you* that translates and assigns meaning to the events of your life; you frame and define your reality.)

NOTB: The relationship between mothers and stepmothers is traditionally considered to be helplessly antagonistic, but it doesn't have to be. How can the Ten Zen Seconds (TZS) method help reduce those nasty feelings that mother and stepmothers often feel toward one another?

EM: Each can come to an interaction between them calmer and more grounded by using the incantations as centering charms. Let's say that you have a phone conversation coming up with your "adversary." The first thing to do is to incant "I am completely stopping," so that you get the chance to quiet your roiling thoughts and your roiling nerves and calmly prepare yourself to listen and to say what you need to say.

Next you might try incanting "I feel supported," to put it in your head and your heart that you are not completely alone in your dealings with "this other woman" and that you have internal and external resources available to you. Then you might try incanting "I embrace this moment" to remind yourself that your intention is to be present, that you are not frightened of the interaction, and that, for the sake of the child involved and for the sake of your own sense of self, you intend to be present in this conversation. Any—and all—of the incantations can be used to "put yourself in the right place" to interact with another human being.

NOTB: Some of the hairier issues that often arise in the mother-stepmother territory are anger, territoriality, and guilt. How can the TZS approach help with those?

EM: Let's take these one at a time. A great way of working with anger is by incanting "I am open to joy"; it is very hard to be angry and joyful at the same time! If you would actually like to not be angry—if, that is, you aren't attached to your anger and holding on to it for dear life—then announcing your intention to be happy can go a long way to dissipate anger.

With territoriality, there are often specific actions that you need to take so that there are clear agreements between all concerned, agreements about visits, rules, and so on, and here incanting "I am taking action" can prove a useful and powerful way to ready yourself to get these agreements made, as can incantation ten, "I am equal to this challenge."

In dealing with guilt, the most important incantation is incantation seven, "I am free of the past," as a great deal of our guilt is about something in the past, as opposed to something ongoing. There are things that you may want to do in the present that serve as correctives to things done in the past, but that is different from feeling guilty about the past and feeling burdened by that guilt. Incanting "I am free of the past" can go a long way to moving you from past-looking to present-being.

NOTB: So how does one do this, especially on the fly? Do you have to be some kind of Zen master?

EM: The first step is to go through the twelve incantations, slowly and mindfully, and find the one or two that feel most useful and resonant. It is very difficult to incorporate all twelve in a regular way into your life, but it isn't hard at all to incorporate one, two, or even three.

HELP YOU CAN USE LATER

If you need help decompressing or recovering from tension or a confrontation, here are a few things (from the ethereal to the physical) that you can do afterward, either over the long term, or simply as needed.

Cognitive therapy—assessing the accuracy of your thoughts

We talked about listening to your thoughts before. Now you get to put them to the test of accuracy. Examine "errors" in your thinking to see if your thoughts are distorted or unrealistic. Our thoughts often paint situations in broad strokes, overgeneralizing and magnifying both positives and negatives.

Try this: Grab a pen and some paper. If there's a situation in particular you're struggling with, see if you can remember one frozen moment, one simple snapshot from that experience. Take a few deep breaths and tap into your feelings. Listen to your thoughts and write them down. Write down a few more. Keep going until you feel complete—cover yourself, the other person, your relationship, and what you expect to happen. Don't censor yourself. Even if your thoughts are startlingly critical, vindictive, or mean-spirited, write them down. No one will be reading this but you.

Now, come back to the present moment. Let's look at your mental dialogue from a distance and see what you're really saying to yourself. Consider one statement at a time. Ask yourself:

- Is this true, false, or I don't know? Something might feel true but still be inaccurate.
- Push back a little when you're uncertain. Really? Do I absolutely know this is true? Do any exceptions exist? If even one exception exists, it's not true.
- How often are you using the words "always" and "never"? Those are tip-offs that your thoughts are exaggerated. How often are you blaming someone else or yourself?

- What are you left with at the end? Often, the only thing we know for sure is how we feel, and that's it!
- Remember, your emotions lead to behavior, and your behavior creates results. Are the grains you're feeding into the hopper high quality? It matters.

MAKING IT MORE REAL

Let's consider an example. Maxine the Mom has just opened her daughter's gym bag by the front door and seen that her daughter's gym shorts were once again left over at Stephanie the Stepmom's house. She blames Stephanie for this, instead of her own daughter, because she specifically asked Stephanie to make *sure* these came home with her daughter, since they are the only pair she will wear. Maxine angrily zips the bag shut.

Here's what's going through her head:

"Doesn't she ever listen? Apparently not! You can't tell her anything. I'll bet she did this on purpose. All she really cares about is herself anyway. She's always going on and on about her stupid new job, as if she's the first person in the world to ever run her own business—what an idiot. Everybody can see that but her. Why Jeff ever married her is a mystery to me."

Any of that sound familiar? How many of those statements are unequivocally and absolutely true? Any of them? Maxine probably feels angry, indignant, and put-upon while she's thinking these thoughts, but that still doesn't make them *true*.

Do you think these thoughts help calm her or stir her up? Do they help her brainstorm a constructive course of action to deal with her problem?

Gooey monsters

For another perspective on validating the truth of your thoughts, consider author Eckhardt Tolle's ideas on the ego and something he calls the "pain-body." To paraphrase, most of what we think of ourselves and the world is really an arbitrary creation of an ego that's heavily invested in itself. Your ego cares about getting ahead, being superior, and creating drama for more opportunities to succeed and dominate. Can you see this in other people? Can you see it in yourself?

These ideas are *greatly* oversimplified, but Tolle suggests that the answer to freedom lies in returning your consciousness back to observing yourself. Are you living from a place of ego? Are you unconsciously enjoying the drama? When you observe the ego in action, you break the link between you and your automatic behavior.

More than just "ohhmmmm"

Meditation has come a long way; it's no longer the bastion of gurus in India, striving for enlightenment on mountaintops. There's an abundance of scientific evidence touting the benefits of meditation, particularly when it comes to "resetting" your autonomic nervous system.

But first, a tiny science lesson. The autonomic nervous system has two parts: the parasympathetic mode, which favors rest and repair (think of parachutes helping you float gently back down to earth); and the sympathetic nervous system, which is activated by stress, for fight-or-flight responses. When you spend too much time tense, worried, and revved up, you're making your body lean too heavily on your sympathetic nervous system, instead of dipping into both parts, as it should. Not only do you pull energy away from your immune system, but such an imbalance can lead to an overall feeling of frazzled nerves and fatigue.

Take up meditation and you'll also be bringing down your heart rate and blood pressure. It can be as simple as sitting somewhere with your eyes closed and listening to your breath. No mantras necessary.

How to feel better when you're in the middle of a tough situation

Here's a tip for tackling your problems in advance. Wrestle them down to the ground with rational thinking and watch your level of confidence and hope for a solution rise.

1. Get the big-picture perspective on the issue.

   Read up on the issue, ask people you know about it, and look up information online.

2. Determine where you want to go.

   What is your goal here? To transform the problem at its core? To simply change your experience of the problem?

   Ask open-ended questions, such as "How do I create ___?" or "What's the best way to do ____?" and see what pops into your mind.

3. Amass tools.

   Gather up and collect any and all information that shows you how to get closer to where you want to go.

   Be creative—look in surprising places for this information, such as animal-behavioral techniques for modifying unpleasant human behavior, or fields such as neuroscience, psychology, and medicine—whatever you can think of that might apply.

4. Experiment with suggested steps, techniques, or exercises.

5. See what happens.

   Step back and assess your results.

   Determine adjustments to make and decide on your next goal.

6. Repeat the steps until you reach your goal

Lastly, we come to the sheer joy of discharging tension with your *body*.

Shake your booty

Exercise can make you feel so much better. For the most part, it's free; it can actually be fun (honest), and doing it for even five minutes makes a difference. Best of all, it diffuses stress like a magic little pill, without side effects! Here are a few things to keep in mind.

Find something you love to do and enjoy. It might take some experimenting before you really stumble upon something that makes you say "Ahhhh . . ." at the same time that you're grunting and sweating away, but the combination is irresistible. If you hate working out at gyms, then don't go. Get outside. Explore and experiment.

Don't worry about how you look or seem. So you feel like you're spilling out of your clothes, or like you're not even sure what clothes you "should" be wearing. Who cares? Feeling stupid and feeling bad about your body are probably the main reasons people don't take up exercise or stick with it. Just remember: Mortification is a temporary experience.

Find something cheap to do that's close to home. Can you make it fun with music you love? Does yoga appeal? Weight-lifting? Are there hiking trails around you? Places to run, ride a bike, or shoot hoops? Be creative. There are lots of things you can do with a pair of tennis shoes.

Find other friends to do it with, if possible. Sometimes, this makes all the difference between fear, drudgery, and procrastination—and a shared learning curve, a good laugh, and, ultimately, commitment.

Do it on a regular basis. Face it, you're always going to be tired or have other things you could be doing. The secret trick about exercise is that once you start doing it consistently, it energizes you. Exercise is the gift that keeps on giving.

Don't do it on a regular basis. Just like anything in life, your routine, time, and wherewithal will falter. Even if you have a few bouts of non-exercise, lasting even weeks or months, trust that you'll always come back to it, because you'll miss how good it makes you feel.

Do it on a tiny basis. Even if you can only get down on the floor and stretch for seven minutes, or jog in place for ten—even if you can only hop on your bike for a quick jaunt, or have time to do a fifteen-minute walk—do it. Your body will thank you and your monkey-mind will especially thank you.

WHAT ABOUT THE MAN?

Is he stoking the fires of conflict between you or trying to stay out of the fray?

If you're his wife, let him know that sometimes the conflict between you and the other woman really wears on you and is taking a toll. Ask for his help to make her a non-subject at times so you can take care of yourself. The health of your own marriage depends upon it. Ask for his help to "keep it clean" between you and vent upon occasion to his friends instead of to you. This may be tough, since a lot of wives are the primary source of emotional support for their husbands.

If you're the mom, do your best to separate any leftover baggage you may still have with him from your relationship with the stepmom. This may sound impossible, but the more you see the stepmom as her own person and not simply a twin to your ex, the better your chances for creating something new with her.

OTHER IDEAS TO TRY

If you're still feeling stumped by problems that are wearing you down, here are a few "let's throw something at the wall and see what sticks" ideas:

- Let some time pass. Step back and put the issue out of your mind. When the intensity fades, come back to it later, if possible.
- Zen acceptance. Let go and just accept that this is reality right now. Surrender to *what is* and stop fighting so hard. Are you trying to change the unchangeable?
- Go back to your dreams to refuel. Remember the benefits you were shooting for in Chapter Three and use them to motivate you.
- Give thanks for what *does* work. Value what you have and stop focusing on the negatives. The more attention you give your problems, the bigger they seem.
- Escapism! Getting away from it all is sometimes a really good idea. Go to the movies, read a book, do something new and different with a friend.
- Therapy. The value of a committed, listening ear cannot be underestimated. Look into free or low-cost options if finances are a concern.

- Friends. They get to be mentioned on this list twice, because they're that good. Call or meet with a supportive friend who has your best interests at heart and will not inadvertently fan the flames of conflict.
- Visualization. Spend some time imagining happy outcomes and scenarios, even if you have no idea how to get there. Just allow yourself to daydream and create some positive mojo that will lurk in your subconscious.

As you can see from some of our suggestions, a fair amount of your stress is actually self-generated! This doesn't mean you're doing things wrong or that you're to "blame"—everyone struggles with challenges. What it *does* mean is that there's more power in your hands than you realize. Increase your abilities to weather any storm and your perspective changes, your triggers change—and your relationships follow.

EXTRA REASSURANCE

If you're really, really struggling, break your life down into smaller chunks. Go hour by hour, and day by day (from managing the morning, to the afternoon, and then the evening). After all, the future never really gets here, does it? The future is just like a carrot being held out if front of you on a stick, constantly moving, constantly being replaced by new details, new worries. So stop looking at the carrot and deal with what's right in front of your face: your present moments! Get the smaller pieces of your life right and the bigger ones will start to come together, too. And make sure to get enough sleep.

Start out with small changes and see where it gets you. If you get nowhere, take a breather, then try again. Monitor your self-talk: Is this the stuff of tragedy, or a shrug and *enh,* moving on? Can you put yourself in the other woman's shoes and imagine what she might be feeling?

Where is it you're trying to go? Consider how high up on the scale of cooperation you're shooting for. What would you consider a success? It's going to be different for everyone. Movement for some might be an exchange of tight grimaces at the front door, whereas before, no one ever even got out of the car for a kid pickup, she just laid on the horn with anger. Improvement for others might be a heartfelt talk on the phone about Lily's grades, Timmy's depression, or Sarah's pot-smoking.

What would be progress for you? And if it's hard, will you keep trying?

Let's gauge where you are with some of the ideas we discussed in this chapter. Ready for some fun?

Quiz: Where are you with your current coping skills?
Circle the most appropriate answer for you.

1. Using deep breaths to slow myself down:
   - a. Makes me dizzy.
   - b. Is too esoteric for my tastes.
   - c. Really actually works.

2. Listening to my thoughts and evaluating their effectiveness:
   - a. Bores me just reading about it.
   - b. Sounds too technical and dry.
   - c. Sounds intriguing and perhaps enlightening.

3. Utilizing calming incantations/affirmations in the moment, as needed:
   - a. Wait—I don't even know what an affirmation is!
   - b. Is only for those new-agey type people.
   - c. Is a welcome addition to my stress-reduction toolbox.

4. Planning to handle my ongoing problems through careful planning and research:
   - a. Who can be bothered?
   - b. Do I look like Martha Stewart?
   - c. I'll do whatever it takes to get somewhere better with all this stress.

5. Exercising to release tension:

      a. Sounds like too much trouble.

      b. I'm not much of an athlete.

      c. Sounds worth the effort—sign me up.

Scoring Guide

If you answered mostly a's, you might be too quick to dismiss new ideas without giving them serious consideration first. What else might you be missing?

If you answered mostly b's, you may feel resistant to anything that you don't already identify with. Is it time to shake up your self-image a bit?

If you answered mostly c's, you're well on your way to living a long and happy life. We commend you!

JOURNAL

So how'd you do? What would you like to change when it comes to how you deal with stress and conflict? Are there any ideas in this chapter that you're considering? What can you do to get the ball rolling?

_____

_____

_____

_____

_____

_____

_____

_____

_____

_____

_____

_____

_____

_____

_____

RESOURCES TO EXPLORE

Books
- *Ten Zen Seconds,* by Eric Maisel
- *The Power of Now Exercises,* by Eckhardt Tolle
- *Loving What Is,* by Katie Bryon

Web sites
- The Happiness Project (www.happiness-project.com/)
- How to Meditate (www.how-to-meditate.org/)
- Taming Your Gremlin (www.tamingyourgremlin.com/)

AS WE LEAVE THE CHAPTER

You've gotten better at tending to yourself when you're having a tough time. Now you're going to set your sights outward and focus on the children. How can you use the progress you've made and sense of partnership with the other woman to support the kids? How can you lean on connections you've created to help them be the best selves they can be? That's where we're heading next.

9
Strengthen
(Bringing Out the Best in the Kids)

A COMMON HORIZON

Enough about the problems between the two women! All children or stepchildren deserve to have adults in their lives who are truly invested in helping them expand their current horizons. They deserve parents who are excited about helping them live a life of passion, curiosity, engagement, and service in the outside world that deepens and enriches their experience of the world inside. Regardless of the problems you've had (and still may have) with the mother or stepmother, we ask you to change your focus from the two of you to the kids. How can you create the happiest children possible? Aren't they the reason you're both involved in each other's lives in the first place? Who knows, having this goal in common might be the one thing that actually brings you together for the first time.

A LOOK BACK FROM US

Jennifer: Over the years, I've tried to encourage whatever passions and interests my two daughters seem to have. There's nothing like helping your children fall in love with some interest or activity and then watching them soar with it, all on their own. We've had our share of successes (mural painting, manga art, photography, bookworm-ism, knitting, traveling), comedic disasters (traveling again, as well as pets— think rabbits, rats, flying squirrels, and enormous dogs), and annoying inconveniences (downloaded songs that crippled my computer).

There were a few experiments where the children were absolutely *certain* that this was something they knew they wanted to do for the rest of their lives and *please oh please could they do it,* only to have their interest suddenly evaporate as soon as they had direct experience (rowing lessons; life as a graphic designer after visiting one in real life; a few flights in small aircraft that left those of us in the backseat seriously queasy, but not the front). Sometimes you encourage your kids to pursue a hobby because it's something *you* wish you could do, and sometimes you encourage them because you can *so* see the activity being a perfect fit for them and yet . . . they're not interested. I guess it goes both ways.

As a single mom, one of my primary concerns has always been cost. At times, I regretted not being able to consistently afford something my children really seemed to love to do, like horseback riding. Other times, this made me reluctant to even entertain an idea unless I *knew* they were really going to stick with it for good, when realistically, there's no way they can know that without doing it first. Over time, my requirements for making a commitment to something at the outset have eased up as I grew older and gave myself permission to experiment with my own interests and curiosities.

There are the things that your children want to do that totally throw you off kilter or simply scare the living daylights out of you, like traveling to Europe alone when they've just turned seventeen, or transferring to the creative school of their choice in a bad part of town, or spending hundreds of dollars on professional manga markers. For the most part, with some heavy-duty negotiations, it's all worked out.

I've delighted in watching my daughters take off with various obsessions: knit impossibly intricate designs of their own creation, track down online rare books by their favorite authors, discover old music anew, become skilled at art beyond their years, and master Japanese. We've carried armloads of books from the library (and paid too many fines as well!), and listened to beginning electric chord organ, violin, and accordion progress from painful to pleasing. I like thinking that the girls are free to pursue their own quirky interests, and that they know they'll always get vocational support from their self-employed parents and stepmom.

Carol: I think my biggest downfall as a stepmother has been letting my feelings of frustration with my stepdaughters (and their parents) get in the way of my support for them. I tend to roll my eyes when I hear about the next obsession: buying an island, being a pilot, anime . . . . I also tend to ask pointed questions like: "How are you going to pay for that?" or "When are you going to get off the computer and clean up your mess in the kitchen?" Practical stuff. I've been accused of squelching their dreams.

Part of me feels like I am just being realistic with these questions, and part of me knows that I am trying to jolt them into reality in an indelicate way. What's the best way to handle these situations? I don't know. Will I be the same way with my own son? Probably close, but without the eye rolling.

There were a few months, years ago, when we each took the girls out for dinner, individually, one week at a time. All three of us alternated. It was tough for me and I always meant to really *bond* with them in some way by having some deep talk about feelings or whatever . . . but usually we ended up doodling on napkins or chatting about really shallow things.

Looking back to long ago, those times meant the most to me. Not the dinners specifically, but just doing things with the girls. I did quite a few craft projects with them: papier-mache, tie-dye, making paper snowflakes, Easter egg decorating, hanging streamers for parties, etc. When they were younger, it was harder because they just wanted to do the fun part and I ended up doing all the prep work and cleanup. But it was nice just sitting side by side, working on something fun.

We got along well during those times. Throughout the project, we would compliment each other and talk about methods and techniques. All in all, it was a safe, fun, easy way to connect. For me and them both I think.

Now I find little ways to support the kids, which to be honest, as they are now teenagers, sometimes requires a lot of tongue-holding more than anything else! Supporting kids is a lifetime project, with methods that require constant readjustments as they grow and change. But I'm getting better at it . . . .

JOURNAL

Can you relate to any of our experiences? In what ways have you supported your children or stepchildren with their own interests and healthy obsessions?

_____

_____

_____

_____

_____

_____

_____

_____

_____

_____

_____

_____

_____

_____

We all know that children need help to pursue their passions, and yet doing so is not always such a clear-cut proposition.

WHAT MIGHT STAND IN THE WAY

Your partnership is still shaky

If you've made progress and created a more cooperative relationship between you and the other woman, you can draw upon that partnership to work together. If things haven't progressed as you would have liked, this is yet another opportunity for change. We understand your reluctance if your relationship with the other woman is still fragile and unstable. Nevertheless, we're asking you to infuse your relationship with a new sense of purpose . . . and try again. See if you can temporarily set your own concerns and agenda aside, put your heads together, and _brainstorm._

How can you help the kids increase their self-esteem and confidence? What support do they need to strengthen their talents and abilities? How can you help them create a plan for where they want to go?

Guilty as charged

We all know we're supposed to be helping our children lead fascinating, wonderful lives full of projects, learning, and discovery, but often—well—this vision tends to fall by the wayside as we become overwhelmed by the stuff of real life. Show us a parental figure who isn't troubled by a pervasive sense of guilt! You *know* what you should be doing, and yet this was *so much easier to do* with toddlers or young children. You could look ahead a bit at an upcoming stage of development and set out calculated opportunities for success: books they would love, toys that would delight and appeal to a particular "bent" of theirs, predetermined problems for them to resolve and master.

It's all too easy to just let kids be on their own in our work- and consumer-oriented culture—for both women. We're all consumed by the busyness of our lives and if getting the kids out of your hair means they end up, once again, on the computer or Game Boy or watching TV, oftentimes our attitude is, well, it's not ideal, but so be it. Unfortunately, what this ends up turning into is a habit of separation and disconnection, the feeling that we don't really know our kids that well anymore (if ever, if the stepmom stepped into the picture when the kids were older) or really spending much quality time with them.

You might feel guilty *now*, but that doesn't mean you have to stay there. The good thing about mistakes: Once you're willing to acknowledge them in all their gory glory, you're free to fix them.

Not all is smooth on the home front

Let's take a step back and assess your relationship with the kids. What's it like? Is it healthy and sturdy, with flare-ups but subsequent patchups, or is it in need of a major overhaul and some serious therapy? Whether you're the mom or the stepmom, neither position is a guarantee of harmony and closeness—or animosity and distance.

Is there any part of you that doesn't want to do this? Are you worried about not having the time or money, or not gaining the other person's cooperation and having to do this all alone? Do you have ongoing issues with one or more of the children or stepchildren at the moment (or perhaps, always)? Is there any leftover anger or resentments interfering with your faith in them? Do you begrudge them further "indulgences" when they can't even put their dirty dishes away without being asked?

Other challenges are overwhelming

It's not uncommon for children to have intense issues that are sometimes overwhelming and scary for parents to deal with. If you have a child who is suffering from depression or intense anxiety, is experimenting with drugs, promiscuity, or failing school, etc., you may feel like this is the *last thing* you can add to your plate right now. Get help if you need it, but don't put this on the back burner until "after everything else has been resolved." Sometimes helping your children return to that feeling of falling in love with a pet interest may be the one thing that finally "takes" and pulls them back to a place of balance. Even if your children don't seem to *have* an interest in anything these days, harken back to earlier days and see if you can find a subject that still resonates with them. Be persistent and hang in there. Your efforts may remind your children of their importance to you and their ability to move through difficult times back into a place of joy and curiosity.

See if you can relate to any of the following worries and concerns.

Quiz: Where are you with supporting the kids' interests and hobbies?

Choose the most appropriate answer. If you have several children or stepchildren, do the quiz separately for each child.

Money

____ This might cost too much money and end up being a financial black hole.

____ I can figure out how to do this on a budget, or without spending much money at all.

Responsibility

____ They never finish anything as it is, why should I give them even more stuff to leave lying around?

____ Maybe they'll take this and run with it if they're really psyched about it.

The right time

____ I'll only let them do this *after* they consistently do their chores and do better in school.

____ I understand the importance of engagement and passion and will try to help them create a balance between joy and responsibility.

Why should I?

____ My current connection with the kids is rocky at the moment—I'll wait until things get better first.

____ Even if we don't get along, I'm willing to step up and support them, despite my unresolved negative feelings.

Time

____ How can I find one more spare moment in my already overwhelmed schedule?

____ I'll find a way to invest the time now, so I can create a happy child with a brighter future.

Commitment

____ I'll only support an interest if I know that this is what they're going to do professionally for the rest of their lives.

____ I understand that interests and hobbies come and go, just as my own interests have changed over the years.

Freedom of choice

____ I'll only do it if they let me have a say in what they should be doing!

____ I'll support their (legal, healthy, nonviolent) subject choices, even if it's not my subject preference.

How'd you do? If you scored mainly first sentences, read on for more inspiration. If you scored mostly second sentences, congratulations! You're well on your way to creating happier children.

WHAT ABOUT THE MAN?

Now let's take a look at another player in this equation: the husband/ ex-husband.

The father may have some worries of his own. He may worry that he's going to be asked to spend even more money, on top of child support. He may worry about the possibility of collaboration jeopardizing the separation between households, something most men usually desire (addressed in earlier chapters). He may worry that he doesn't have the time to devote to something "extra" on top of work, existing family life, etc.

Again, sometimes we're reluctant to make big changes if we first have to see how poorly we were doing it before. It's possible that taking a close look at this issue might make the father feel guilty or anxious about how he hasn't done this stuff in the past.

Emphasize the positives. If an imbalance existed before, remind him that now is his opportunity to rectify that imbalance. Focus on the present possibilities, let the rest go, and let the past be the past. Know that what you're trying to do here is come together as a team to set the stage for happiness and success in the kids' lives.

Men are very task- and goal-oriented. Call upon his insights into his children's personalities, strengths, and known issues. He has a unique understanding of them that's different from the mother or stepmother—ask him to put this knowledge to work in the service of his children.

And remind him of the possible *benefits*.

WHY DO THIS?

The good stuff

Supporting your kids is what love in action looks like in a family. You create a warm, nurturing environment where they are free to explore and experiment within the confines of a family nest. Hobbies, healthy obsessions, and interests help your children or stepchildren develop a sense of mastery and competence, which in turn develops other important skills such as persistence, flexibility, focus, concentration, and problem-solving. You also help your children or stepchildren see a process or sequence through until the very end and gain a sense of completion, an experience that's a bit rare in these times of immediate gratification. Passionate interests are great practice for the real world, and for helping your children or stepchildren internalize the skills needed to create a happy future.

Potential payoffs

Sure, it takes forethought, planning and purposeful analysis to address the needs of our children, but look at what happens if you make the effort. You let the kids know that you *see* them. You're taking the time and devoting the attention to search deep inside their psyches—you value the things that are important to them. When people feel validated, they often feel inspired. And who knows? You might even end up with less arguing, less tension, and more cooperation in your household—and happier, more cooperative children!

So what *are* your child's or stepchild's interests and talents?

Visualization

Take a moment and close your eyes. Imagine how you want the children or stepchildren in your life to feel. Remember what it's like to lose track of time doing something you love? Imagine the children feeling this way. Imagine them feeling alive and engrossed, engaged—*free*. See their happiness, their intense absorption, their focus, and passion. See them sharing their insights and discoveries with excitement with their friends and family. See their self-confidence growing and their spirits thriving.

JOURNAL

What did you imagine? Did anything surprise you? Do you have any new insights into potential challenges or successes? What information do you now feel compelled to act upon?

_____

_____

_____

_____

_____

_____

_____

_____

_____

_____

Let's take a closer look at the tools we can use to accomplish this vision.

EXAMINE WHAT THEY NEED

Pondering possibilities

First, consider these questions. What are your child's or stepchild's strengths and skills? How can you play to them? What are some hobbies or activities that would help them develop in positive ways? What feeds your children's souls? How can you support them in cultivating leadership, self-esteem, social skills, compassion, and being of service? How can you create opportunities for them to succeed? Look at their physical, artistic, intellectual, and creative talents—can you see their potential?

Ask them!

Have a conversation with them and see what they say. Take them out to lunch or dinner or take advantage of time in the car. Set your preconceived perceptions about them aside. Really listen and avoid interruptions. Ask them:

- What do you enjoy doing? What do you love?
- What makes you effortlessly happy?
- What makes time fly for you?

If you're still stumped, here are two more questions to privately ponder. What are their inner gifts, however hidden or dormant? And… if you won the lottery and could give them a wonderful surprise where money was no object, what would it be?

Now it's time to take action.

FIGURE OUT HOW TO MAKE IT HAPPEN

Work together as adults

Invite the other adults to brainstorm collaboratively with you (and remember the pitfalls of one-upmanship or refresh your memory by returning to Chapter Two). Have a meeting or talk together on the phone. Keep the emphasis on creating happy, thriving children, and not on solving their "problems."

Allow for hits and misses

Be willing to let the kids experiment with lots of interests. Let them make the process *theirs*. When it comes to curiosity, there are no failures. Balance forays into newness with a reasonable budget and let them try things out at their own pace, without you hovering over them.

At some point, you can evaluate whether this is something the children are really into, and whether they're finding a balance between their new interests and schoolwork, household responsibilities, friends, and so on.

Assess your resources

Look into resources online and at the library. Are there any local, online groups you can join? Such groups are often great sources of information for supplies at cost, as well as specialized classified ads and opportunities to barter or swap.

Consider your day and find a small pocket of time when you can focus on helping this endeavor succeed. Are there role models or mentors who might also be willing to help, such as friends or colleagues, teachers, or professionals in your area? Are there any classes or workshops that might be perfect for your child?

Keep the benefits in mind

This doesn't all have to be some huge, over-the-top show of support. Focus on creating small, cumulative happy moments in your child's life, solidify a positive vision for the future, and take it one level of development at a time.

Status Check

Are you willing to try now? Will you make the commitment? Where are you with the following elements necessary for success? For each statement, fill in the bar to rate your level of agreement and readiness, as shown in the sample scale.

Sample scale:

| Zip/zilch | In the middle | I'm raring to go! |

Time

Attention

Patience

Acceptance of "failures"

[ ]

Listening well

[ ]

Following the child's lead

[ ]

Budget

[ ]

ONE LAST MOTIVATOR

Working on this step together is one of the most important things you can do to create an extended family that's stable, strong, and caring. You potentially mend some of the damage inherent in divorce and provide a framework for success that's similar to what's found in a nuclear family. Give it your all and watch your children bloom.

EXTRA REASSURANCE

Knowing when to move on . . .

Your efforts to involve the father and the other woman may fall upon deaf ears. Sometimes it's best to know when to cut your losses. If this is where you find yourself, resolve to create the happiest version of *your* family possible. You don't have to do it from a space of competitiveness either—simply keep your focus on the children or stepchildren and what makes them *come alive.* The other adults may come around once they see the results of your hard work.

EXERCISE: WHO ARE THESE LITTLE PEOPLE AND WHAT WOULD SUPPORT THEM?

Let's get specific. Assess what would best support your children's or stepchildren's confidence, growth, and development. Make sure to consider a wide range of possible topics (physical, artistic and creative, intellectual) and potential resources in the form of existing materials and people (mentors or consultants in the form of acquaintances, colleagues, local programs). Use a separate piece of paper if you need more room to write.

Child: _____

Area of Interest/Topic: _____

Budget: _____

Potential Resources Needed: _____

_____

_____

_____

Available Resources: _____

_____

_____

_____

First Action Items: _____

_____

_____

_____

Child: _____

Area of Interest/Topic: _____

Budget: _____

Potential Resources Needed: _____

_____

_____

_____

Available Resources: _____

_____

_____

_____

First Action Items: _____

_____

_____

_____

Child: _____

Area of Interest/Topic: _____

Budget: _____

Potential Resources Needed: _____

_____

_____

_____

Available Resources: _____

_____

_____

_____

First Action Items: _____

_____

_____

_____

RESOURCES TO EXPLORE

Books

- *The Good Enough Child: How to Have an Imperfect Family and Be Perfectly Satisfied,* by Brad E. Sachs, Ph.D.
- *The Shelter of Each Other: Rebuilding Our Families,* by Mary Pipher, Ph.D.
- *Nurturing Good Children Now: 10 Basic Skills to Protect and Strengthen Your Child's Core Self,* by Dr. Ron Taffel with Melinda Blau

Web sites

- How to Make Stuff (www.howtomakestuff.com/)
- Martha Beck (www.marthabeck.com/)
- Zen Habits (www.zenhabits.net)

AS WE LEAVE THE CHAPTER

Now we head into the last chapter of the book and set our sights on celebrating all the ways we've made progress on this strange and unconventional journey to wholeness and harmony. How can you embrace each of the members of your "extended family" in all their flawed and human glory? You're about to find out!

10

Celebrate and Acknowledge

(Anytime is Springtime)

SHAKING HANDS OVER THE FENCE

*Have you ever had a big, overwhelming project you needed to tackle and as you went along, you kept saying to yourself, "Oh my gawd, I'm still so far from being finished, this is going to **kill** me! I'll **never** get there!"? What effect did this have on your energy level? Your motivation?*

If all the unresolved issues between you and the other woman still feel like a piano dangling from a fishing line over your head, we want you to take a step back for a breather. In this chapter, we're going to recognize the insights you've gained, the changes you've made, and the connections you've created thus far in your journey from acrimony to accord. That's the stuff that will keep you going in the face of new challenges.

*Can you take comfort in the fact that you're doing something rare and revolutionary? That you're ahead of the curve? The cultural norm? If you're reading this book, **you are!** So celebrate even minor achievements and build a sense of family wherever you can find it. By creating a bridge from your family to theirs, **both** families become stronger, more resilient, and, most important, more stable.*

A LOOK BACK FROM US

Carol: The last few years we've spent our Christmases together: me, David, the girls, and Jen (and J. now too); one big, weird family.

The first time it happened was kind of impromptu. The girls were staying with us, and I believe we had gone out to visit my family for Christmas Eve. When Jen and her boyfriend came to pick up the girls on Christmas Day, they brought their presents inside for the girls to open. I can't remember why now. They had already opened their presents from us, so I felt a bit awkward watching them open more, with nothing from us.

Jen gave the girls fewer but fancier presents. While we had shopped mostly for toys and clothes, Jen got them little keepsakes and fancy art supplies. The girls loved it.

I felt out-done.

The next year, because David felt it was important for the kids, and since I didn't see a way out of it(!), we planned to share Christmas morning together. We cooked a big breakfast at our house and they brought over all their presents. We all opened them together, even ones from us to Jen and vice versa.

It was nice. My wall came down some.

The next year I think was when we got J., and I rebuilt my wall a little bit. I thought, "This is my family: me, David, the girls, and J. I don't want to share it." But David talked me into softening up and at that point, Jen and I were getting along pretty well, so we did the breakfast and gifts thing again. And it was actually pretty nice. My wall came down more. . . .

Now we do it every year (unless someone is out of town . . . and then we generally postpone it). The difference now is that we do it with real feeling. We all genuinely want to share this special time of year with each other. It's important to all of us.

We also generally get together for all birthdays and other family events. And sometimes even an impromptu breakfast, lunch, or dinner. We talk and laugh . . . and sometimes cry and yell . . . but it's always over stuff that needs to be worked out.

We're honestly a big, albeit weird, family. And it's really good.

Jennifer: I'd long had this idea in my head for some kind of coming-of-age "ceremony" for S. and then later, for M. Chalk it up to reading too many books on mythology and the power of rituals to positively shape your subconscious and your future.

At first, I thought we'd do it when she turned sixteen, but that didn't happen. Then I thought I'd do it later, when she graduated. But really, what pushed the idea to the fore was her graduating early and leaving for foreign lands (Europe) on her own.

What I had *in mind* was a group of female elders, sitting around, telling the unvarnished truth about a variety of topics—ones that grown-ups dealt with—like life purpose, sex, relationships, responsibility, money. I imagined women who had known her all (or most) of her life sitting around telling stories— relaying near misses, lessons learned the hard way, things they'd wish they'd known long ago. I was hoping to spare her some of our mistakes and give her a shortcut to some of our hard-earned insights.

Those same nuggets of wisdom could also go in a book. I'd gather everyone's tales beforehand and we'd give it to S. during the party as a gift. I envisioned a gathering full of laughter, juicy details, lots of love, and an easy intimacy in the air.

What ended up happening was . . . *slightly different.*

Carol and I brainstormed the guest list and whittled down the number of topics from fifteen to ten. We planned the food, who would make what, and I started tackling the house.

It was going to be women only so we could really let it all hang out, but David felt a bit left out, so we made him the honorary man-guest. If this was going to be some kind of big, meaningful send-off for his daughter, he didn't want to just be at home, wondering what was going on.

What became evident after I sent out the invitations was how squirmy people felt about their little "writing assignment." Several folks left it until the last minute. When I finally did my writing, I saw why! This task was *hard*—even embarrassing. *This* cliché crap was the best I could do?

Leave it to Carol and David to tactfully bring it to my attention that S. *probably* wouldn't really enjoy or appreciate a roomful of adults giving her what would *probably* feel like a bunch of advice. It all seemed so nice and glow-y in theory, but in practice, would likely feel forced and awkward. So we dropped the "ritualistic" part of it and simply focused on the book. Carol's mom, Sandra, made a beautiful handmade one (creativity runs in the family), and we put the whole thing together one evening, a few days before the party.

So the day of the gathering finally arrived. We had four enormous dogs in the house, more food than we could possibly eat, and since S.'s friends had been here the past several days in a nonstop slumber party, they came too. The various "elders" arrived (decked out in feathered headdresses and bejeweled canes—kidding), and so did J., S.'s little brother. It was quite the raucous event.

No ceremonies.

No rituals.

Just an acknowledgment that S. was about to take off on a journey out into the big, wide world. Some talk of where she was going, what she'd like to do. But no pronouncements from on high. Just boatloads of fantastic food, wine, and a fancy, crystal punch dispenser that looked like it was imported from Russia (thanks, Mom!). And a few mumbled words from me as I handed over the book, about how much we all loved her and were going to miss her, but how excited we also all were for her. There was a murmuring of agreement and lots of beaming, adoring faces.

Perhaps the most inadvertently ritualistic touch came from S.'s little sister M. herself, in an impromptu idea that she came up with all on her own. For about two days before the party, M. worked furiously, cutting up long strips of paper to be folded into beautiful little paper stars. She used patterned paper (that kid could work magic with *dirt*) and got the stars "started" for people. Then she printed out instructions for everyone, asking them to write a secret wish, hope, or special saying for S. She bought her a tiny cardboard treasure chest to store the stars in (something small and light to fit in her backpack) and set out pens, books to write on, and a little glass jar to collect the stars on a pretty tray. We were to find out later that S. doled these stars out to herself when she felt lonely or homesick in Europe.

The party was loud, crazy, and chaotic, but it was also wonderfully *us*. We each had our part to play and couldn't have done it without each other. As far as imparting some sort of life-changing maxims that S. would treasure forever, well, I suppose some plans just rightfully fall by the wayside. I took comfort in the fact that S. has a good head on her shoulders and knew she was surrounded by love. That would be enough . . . .

Even if you aren't at the point of throwing parties with the other woman (yet), let's take a look at how far you've come over the course of this book.

JOURNAL: FROM HERE TO THERE

Take a moment, center yourself, and let your mind run through the gamut of experiences you've had in your own "extended family." Remember what it was like in the beginning, when things were completely new with the other woman? How have you changed? What's easier? What used to be a problem, but is no longer? (Even little things count as progress, such as smiles, eye contact, or mumbled hellos.) We'll take an even closer look at these changes further in the chapter.

_____

_____

_____

_____

_____

_____

_____

_____

_____

_____

_____

_____

_____

_____

_____

_____

_____

_____

_____

_____

_____

_____

_____

_____

_____

_____

_____

_____

_____

_____

HOW FAR YOU'VE COME

Keeping your spirits up—the value of recognition

Here's a question for you: how good are you at acknowledging *yourself* for a job well done? We've spent an *entire* book outlining the ways that mother/stepmother relationships can be persistently difficult and draining. But you stuck with it, and you hung in there, and you even made it to the (almost) end of this book! Was it difficult to answer the journal questions above? Were you struggling to give yourself enough credit? Do you make it a habit to validate yourself for your hard work on a regular basis?

Recognition is the fuel that keeps us going. It lets you know your efforts *matter,* they make a difference. Often, we think we don't deserve acknowledgment and praise until a situation or issue is completely handled from start to finish. But this mom/stepmom scenario isn't something that necessarily has a solid beginning or end, so how about doling out a few kudos in the moment?

Close your eyes, take a few cleansing, slow, deep breaths, and give yourself credit for the effort you've put into improving this relationship with the other woman, for strengthening your entire family environment.

Acknowledge yourself for being willing to:

- consider your own behavior honestly and assess the results you were creating
- own your own crap as we asked you to look at unpleasant truths that you would have happily ignored
- open your heart and mind
- practice the art of forgiveness, kindness, and compassion
- brainstorm helpful strategies for communication and collaboration
- experiment with new behavior
- pick yourself back up when you fell down and take responsibility for putting yourself back together again, without being a victim

We acknowledge you too! This is some of the hardest stuff in the world to deal with on an emotional level, and you've been right there with us, working hard. *Way to go!*

Spreading the love

While you're at it, how about throwing a few accolades out there for other folks, too? Often, we go for years, longing to be thanked for things that others think we already know or understand, when in reality, hearing it *said* would make such a huge difference. Express your appreciation for efforts you've seen the other woman make, along with the kids, and your husband, or ex. Tell them what you've been meaning to say but keep forgetting. Push past the resistance you have, the fear that doing this will put you in a submissive position.

It might be scary to make yourself vulnerable this way, but by now, we're sure you've had plenty of practice in reaching out. Even if your efforts are met with a less-than-ideal reaction, would you be willing to try it and just see what happens?

WHAT ABOUT THE MAN?

In each chapter, we've had a separate section examining the husband or ex-husband's influence upon the relationship between the two women and often cautioned both sides about the potential for increased conflict. Now, we simply want you to focus on his positive contributions. And if you're the ex-wife—yes—surely you can find *something* to acknowledge.

Make sure he gets the ego strokes, too! Keep the focus on what you've both accomplished and not existing, ongoing problems. Thank him for his support, his understanding, his flexibility, his concern for the kids, and for adding to family harmony.

Sometimes it's easier to imagine doing something when you have the words to say in front of you. Along those lines, here are some things to consider saying, if they feel true for you. Feel free to tweak and rearrange as necessary:

For stepmoms:

- Thank you for supporting me in reducing my stress and helping me to improve my relationship with your ex-wife, even when it was difficult for you.
- Thank for you for holding your tongue when I wanted additional "artillery" to make her wrong.
- Thank you for trying to understand my unique pain in not getting to have our relationship be our own special thing that starts off on neutral ground.
- Thank you for seeing that my pain and struggles are not necessarily any sort of rejection of your children, but more a function of our situation.

For moms:

- Thank you for supporting me in improving my relationship with your wife, even though it must have felt weird or even threatening to you.
- Thank you for not turning your relationship into a situation where it was always "your two against my one."
- Thank you for keeping our children's best interests in mind and helping us all to reduce the conflict that is inherent in divorce, remarriage, and stepfamily life.
- Thank you for doing your best to heal your leftover baggage from our divorce and being patient with me as I attempted to heal mine.

Are you getting the hang of this validation thing? Hopefully it's getting easier, even if it's awkward at the beginning. Imagine the look of surprised pleasure on the face of your listener, receiving validation when he wasn't expecting it!

PUTTING CURRENT PROBLEMS IN PERSPECTIVE

What if you're still dragged down by the problems that exist in your family situation? Maybe you feel like the scales are still tipping toward the terrible and things aren't going to change anytime soon . . . .

Well, the reality is that there *are* some pretty entrenched problems built in to these family arrangements. And as we've said all along, there are some things that you're just not going to be able to change or improve. But we'd like to take one last opportunity to help you put those issues into a less personal perspective.

If you're still lamenting any friction you have with the other woman, the children, your husband, or ex-husband, step back for a moment and see if you can assess and understand any *resistance* you might feel from them from a different vantage point. Can you depersonalize it and put it in a different context? Things are usually nowhere near as "about us" as we assume. Is it possible to figure out the reason for distance between you two from a clearer place?

Are the other woman's problems with you also applicable in other areas of her life? Can you detect any suffering underneath her hostile or distancing behavior? Can you return to some of the things you learned in Chapter Four about compassion and apply them here?

For instance, some of the resistance or distance between you and the children may be related to leftover grief from the divorce, whether you're the mother or the stepmother. No matter how much their parents didn't get along, the loss of the original family unit is often devastating to them on a core level. It can be hard to consciously process such a loss. A failure to do so makes it hard for them to fully connect with the other adults, the stepmother in particular, but also their own mother and father. It takes time to travel all the way down through grief and come out the other side. Give the children space, and support them as you're able. Do your best to honor where the children are. And of course, as we've said all along, get professional help if it seems warranted.

Lastly, is there anything you need to make amends for? Do so. Practice the freeing art of "lopsided" apologies where you expect and wait for nothing to come back to you after you say your part. It's a wonderful way to clean up the worries that persistently nag you and quiet your mind. If a situation is really and truly out of your hands and doesn't improve despite your earnest efforts, do your best to just let it go (see Chapter Eight on regrouping if you need a refresher on how to do this).

Creating your own shade under a scorching sun

If you still feel discouraged by how far you have to go to create cooperation and understanding between yourself and the other woman, it's time to up the emphasis on why you *still* have reasons to thank your lucky stars. Consider what you do *not* have to deal with to get you to a more forward-focused mind-set and make the good parts of your life crystal clear.

What are you grateful for? What's working? Go through your life with a magnifying glass and outline it all. Do you give daily thanks for the good stuff? It's a powerful habit to start your day off with, and it can make you feel almost obscenely lucky on a regular basis.

Let's start. For instance, consider your relationship with the other woman, with the children or stepchildren, with your husband or ex-husband:

- Where is there now *patience,* instead of irritation?
- Where is there now *engagement and involvement,* instead of avoidance and distraction?
- Where is there now *support, validation, and acceptance,* instead of lousy listening, criticism, and grudges?
- Where is there now *trust,* instead of suspicion?
- Where is there now *closeness,* instead of distance?
- Where is there now *affection,* instead of formality?
- Where is there now *humor and play,* instead of awkwardness and stiffness?
- Where is there now genuine *love,* instead of coldness and unfamiliarity?

Here's another way to come at the obstacles between you and peace and happiness. Take one of your existing complaints and look at one benefit hidden within the complaint. If you can't see any benefits, then at least look at what the situation is *not.*

For example, if you are the mom and you wish the stepmom had never come into the picture, think of what her existence *does* accomplish. To follow our example, at least your ex isn't the *only* one parenting them. She's an extra pair of hands, another adult watching over them, in addition to your ex. You're well aware of your ex's blind spots as a parent, and you know she makes up for a few of those, as much as you might begrudgingly admit it. Surely, no matter how much you can't stand her, this reality has crossed your mind before, right?

Take this situation and turn it into a statement with a conscious choice involved. The one above would be: I choose to be grateful for my ex-husband's wife because there is another woman in the maternal role watching over my children, even if we disagree on many things. Or: I choose to be grateful because there's another pair of hands helping my children's father do a better job of raising them. Or if you can't say that, you could say something about how your own personal growth is being developed by the challenges you're dealing with the other woman.

Let's say you're the stepmom and you can't stand the ex-wife. Your statement might be something along the lines of: I choose to be grateful for my husband's ex-wife because he learned many things in that marriage that I now benefit from. Or: I choose to be grateful for my husband's ex-wife because she bore him the children whom he loves so much. Or if you can't stomach that, you could try something like: I choose to be grateful for my husband's ex-wife because she inadvertently helps me better define my boundaries for our family.

So the formula goes: *I choose to be grateful for* (short statement of the problem) *because it means that* (positive undeniable reality or absence of a problem that's even worse).

Now you try a few. Coming back to these every so often to see how they're still true—or whether there are new ones to add—can help you keep your head above water when the going gets rough.

I choose to be grateful for_____
because _____
_____.

I choose to be grateful for_____

because _____

_____.

I choose to be grateful for_____

because _____

_____.

A before and after snapshot

Remember the quiz you filled out in the first chapter (p. 24) after you familiarized yourself with some of the more challenging aspects of being stuck with an ex-wife or stepmother in your life? Let's see where you were *before* and compare it to where you are *now* with specific issues and emotions.

Look back to your answers from Chapter One and circle the proper rating in the first column. Then circle the number in the second column that corresponds to your current state. One represents a low level of intensity and ten represents your absolute limit.

Issue	Rating Before	Rating Now
Jealousy	1 2 3 4 5 6 7 8 9 10	1 2 3 4 5 6 7 8 9 10
Territoriality/ Competitiveness	1 2 3 4 5 6 7 8 9 10	1 2 3 4 5 6 7 8 9 10
Anger and Resentment	1 2 3 4 5 6 7 8 9 10	1 2 3 4 5 6 7 8 9 10
Insecurity and Fear	1 2 3 4 5 6 7 8 9 10	1 2 3 4 5 6 7 8 9 10
Sadness and Despair	1 2 3 4 5 6 7 8 9 10	1 2 3 4 5 6 7 8 9 10
Helpless and Overwhelmed	1 2 3 4 5 6 7 8 9 10	1 2 3 4 5 6 7 8 9 10
Denial and Avoidance	1 2 3 4 5 6 7 8 9 10	1 2 3 4 5 6 7 8 9 10
Stress	1 2 3 4 5 6 7 8 9 10	1 2 3 4 5 6 7 8 9 10

And we'll throw in a couple of new ones too.

Issue	Rating Before	Rating Now
Compassion	1 2 3 4 5 6 7 8 9 10	1 2 3 4 5 6 7 8 9 10
Forgiveness	1 2 3 4 5 6 7 8 9 10	1 2 3 4 5 6 7 8 9 10
Empathy and understanding of the other woman's fears and concerns	1 2 3 4 5 6 7 8 9 10	1 2 3 4 5 6 7 8 9 10
Empathy and understanding of your own fears and concerns	1 2 3 4 5 6 7 8 9 10	1 2 3 4 5 6 7 8 9 10

JOURNAL

How'd you do? Is it easier now to see evidence of movement and change within yourself? Do you feel more hopeful about dealing with some of the challenges of your situation? What would you like to continue to working on? How can you acknowledge yourself for the ways in which you've worked hard and grown and changed as a person?

_____

_____

_____

_____

_____

_____

_____

_____

_____

_____

_____

LOOK FOR MORE WAYS TO BOND AND CONNECT

With all the evidence that you've accumulated of your progress in this chapter, are you more willing than ever to build upon your gains? Are you open to getting somewhere even better? Good!

There are some simple but powerful things you can do to get to know all the members of your extended family even better. In Chapter Three, we asked you to daydream about some of the positive possibilities of working together, which included more support for each other as parents, stronger romantic partnerships, and, most important, happier children. Even if it takes some time to get there, be patient and open and do your best to keep a positive outcome in mind.

For tips on reaching out, collaborating, and communicating well, make sure to revisit Chapters Four, Five, and Seven. Here are some ideas to try, if possible:

- *Family dinners or brunches.* Meet at a restaurant so no one has to clean up or meet at someone's house. Make it potluck or take turns hosting.
- *Meet one-on-one with the kids.* Take turns taking the kids out, just the two of you. Shoot for at least once a month and watch your relationship with them change as they feel valued in your eyes.
- *Get together with the other woman and check in.* Meet for coffee, lunch, dinner, or just at the park. Turn to Chapter Four for specifics on how to handle this well.
- *Celebrate birthdays together.* Again, take turns hosting and divvy up the food, drinks, and cake. Only friendly, cheerful behavior is allowed to create the best memories for the kids.
- *Celebrate holidays together.* Try spending a Thanksgiving or Christmas all together at one house or the other (or alternate on different years). We spend Thanksgiving separately and spend Christmas together. We have a decadent, potluck brunch, followed by the opening of presents all together.

JOURNAL

What are you interested in trying? What steps will you take to set this in motion, right now?

_____

_____

_____

_____

_____

_____

_____

_____

_____

_____

_____

Keeping up with household chores

As your journey continues with the other woman, don't forget to keep your emotional house clean on a regular basis. Tend to misunderstandings and mistakes as soon as they happen and you'll eliminate that horrible feeling of having a psychic backlog hanging over your head. Prioritize the things that still need your attention and promise yourself you'll deal with them—then do it!

EXTRA REASSURANCE

Remember, you can still make great strides in creating harmony and peace in your own family even if the other side is unwilling to meet you halfway. After reading this book, you now better understand your own feelings, motivation, and behavior, as well as the other woman's. Use this information to head off conflict, continue to put out feelers for potential cooperation, and calm yourself when things go wrong (see also Chapter Eight). With time and continued patience, you'll strike a balance between wise attempts at reaching out and knowing when to pull back.

RESOURCES TO EXPLORE

Books
- *The 100 Simple Secrets of Happy People: What Scientists Have Learned and How You Can Use It,* by David Niven
- *The Relationship Cure: A 5-Step Guide to Strengthening Your Marriage, Family and Friendships,* by John Gottman
- *Connections: The Threads that Strengthen Families,* by Jean Illsey Clarke

Web sites
- The Gottman Institute (www.gottman.com/)
- SouleMama (www.soulemama.com/)
- Values Parenting (www.valuesparenting.com)

AS WE LEAVE THE CHAPTER (AND THE BOOK)

We'd like to take a moment to say we're mighty impressed. And we're proud of you! You're taking serious and important steps to repair the damage of divorce. After all, if our children are to grow into their most glorious, wonderful selves, how can they do so alone? They need as many people as possible to help them get there. That's why one of the most generous things you can do for the kids is to make room for a bigger sense of family *that works for them.*

Good luck with your continued efforts to create two-family harmony and we wish you well! If you'd like to keep in touch and meet other folks working on the same goals, make sure to visit us online at www.noonesthebitch.com and join the conversation!

Index

A

accountability, 139–54
  benefits of, 145–46
  what stands in the way, 148–49
advice and trained professionals,
    23, 87, 218
anger, 5, 7–8, 46–47, 183
anxiety, fear and insecurity, 5,
    8–9
apologies, 100–102, 218
appreciation and gratitude, 170
The Art of Forgiveness,
    Lovingkindness, and Peace
    (Kornfield), 114
autonomic nervous system, 186
avoidance, 6, 11

B

benefits
  of accountability, 145–46
  to helping children succeed,
    145–46
  partnership between ex-wife/
    stepmom, 58–82
Bonus Families web site, 138
books, resources, 26–27, 57, 82,
    114, 137, 154, 173, 193, 208,
    225
boundaries, 86–89
Brain, Child web site, 82
brainstorming, 130

C

change and uncertainty, 91
The Change Blog web site, 154
charts
  accountability, 144
  self-analysis, 56
  shadow aspect, 56
  who are you accountable
    to, 144
  why it matters, 34
children
  and a cohesive family, 62–63
  and conflict between adults,
    67–68
  and parenting, 70–73
  and rules between houses,
    71–72, 129–34
  support from adults with
    interests and hobbies,
    194–209
cognitive therapy, 184–85
collaboration, 116–38, 223–24
communication, 155–73
  and accountability, 103–11
  body language, 108
  consequences of poor
    communication, 161–66
  dialogue, 125–26
  e-mails, greeting cards,
    telephone, small gift or
    offering, invitations, 106–7
  expressing yourself, 159

family meetings, 169–70

focusing on one issue at a time, 109–10

good communication, 167–68

gossip, 92, 111, 163–66

greetings at the door, 104–6

and husbands, 151–52

inflammatory language, 108

and listening, 108–9, 125, 158–59

and manners, 159–61

words and semantics, 108

compassion, 42, 90–91

competitiveness, 5, 7, 92

conflict, kinds of, 177–78

Connections: The Threads That Strengthen Families (Clarke), 82, 225

consistency, 129–34

coping skills, 92–93, 112

Crucial Conversations: Tools for Talking When Stakes are High (Patterson, Grenny, McMillan and Switzler), 173

D

defensiveness, 122–23, 127–28

denial, 6, 11, 32–33

The DHX: The Doughtie Houses Exchange web site, 138

dialogue, 125–26

Difficult Conversations: How to Discuss What Matters Most (Stone, Patton and Heen), 173

divorce, and remarried couples, 69, 102–3

divorce papers, 19–20

Divorce Poison: Protecting the Parent-Child Bond from a Vindictive Ex (Warshak), 27

Divorcing Daze web site, 173

drama issues, 20

E

ego, 186

exercises

asking for what you want, 168

collaborating with the other woman, 127

supporting the children, 206–8

Ex-Etiquette for Parents: Good Behavior After a Divorce or Separation (Blackstone-Ford and Jupe), 26

external influences, 18–20

F

family meetings, 169–70

finger pointing, 146–47

The Five Things We Cannot Change and the Happiness We Find by Embracing Them (Richo), 114

forgiveness, 89–90

Forgiving web site, 115

The Four Agreements: A Practical Guide to Personal Freedom, A Toltec Wisdom Book (Ruiz), 154

friends and family, 29–30

G

Giving the Love That Heals: A Guide for Parents (Hendrix), 82

The Good Enough Child: How to Have an Imperfect Family and Be Perfectly Satisfied (Sachs), 208

gossip, 92, 111, 163–66

The Gottman Institute web site, 225

grief, sadness and despair, 6, 9–10, 94–96, 218

grievances, 149

grudges, 46

guilt, 183

H

The Happiness Project web site, 193

helplessness and feeling overwhelmed, 6, 10, 23–24, 111

Hendrix, Harville, 134

How to Make Stuff web site, 208

How to Meditate web site, 193

husbands/ex-husbands

actions toward relationship between ex-wife/stepmother, 151–52

and collaboration, 122, 127–29

and communication, 166–67

and defensiveness, 127–28

fears, 73, 93–94

guilt, 128–29

impact and influence on relationship between ex-wife and new wife, 15–17, 73–77, 189, 216–217

as intermediary, 11, 17

privacy issues, 15–16

and stepmother/ex-wife relationship, 43–48

supporting the kids' interests, 201–2

I

inner voices, 179–80

insanity/crazy aggression, 38

insecurity, 5

Interlude Retreat web site, 57

internal actions, 85–96

J

jealousy, 5, 6–7, 16–17

Jung, Carl, 32

K

Keeping Kids Out of the Middle: Child-Centered Parenting in the Midst of Conflict, Separation, and Divorce (Garber), 137

know-it-all, 36

L

legal system, 19–20

lies, 39

listening, 108–9, 125, 158–59

Literary Mama web site, 82
Loving What Is (Bryon), 193

M
Maisel, Eric, interview, 181–83
manipulation and control, 37
manners, 159–61
Martha Beck web site, 208
meditation, 186
Miller, John G., 149
The Miracle of Mindfulness (Nhat Hanh), 154
money issues, 18–19, 23, 28–29, 48–49
motivating factors, 91–92
mourning, 94–96

N
The National Stepfamily Resource Center web site, 27
negative emotions, 45–46
New Conversations web site, 173
Nonviolent Communication: A Language of Life (Rosenberg), 173
No One's the Bitch web site, 27
nuclear families, 69
Nurturing Good Children Now: 10 Basic Skills to Protect and Strengthen Your Child's Core Self (Taffel and Blau), 208

O
The 100 Simple Secrets of Happy People: What Scientists Have Learned and How You Can Use It (Niven), 225

P
parenting
    and adult support, 70–71, 194–209
    and rules between both houses, 71–72, 129–34
    and tough problems, 72–73
parenting wars, 30––31
partnership between ex-wife/ stepmom
    benefits, 58–82, 103
    celebrate and acknowledge, 210–25
    common features, 5–11, 16
    communication, 103–11
    creating one extended family, 77–80
    external actions, 96–115
    external influences, 18–20
    fears about getting along, 78–80
    giving thanks for the good stuff, 219–20
    increasing children's self-esteem and confidence, 194–209
    internal actions, 85–96

more ways to bond and
    connect, 223–24
and parenting, 70–73
payoffs *vs.* costs, 52–55
professional help, 23, 87, 218
putting current problems in
    perspective, 217–21
signaling a change, 106–8
top ten reasons not to get
    along, 34–35
visualizing better
    relationship, 61
passive-aggressive forgetting, 163
passive-aggressive people, 38
Pathway to Happiness web
    site, 82
Peace Is Every Step (Nhat
    Hanh), 150
*Personal Development for Smart
    People: The Conscious
    Pursuit of Personal Growth*
    (Pavlina), 137
Personal Growth Planet web
    site, 154
Pick the Brain web site, 115
plotting and planning, 37
Postcards from Splitsville web
    site, 138
*The Power of Now: A Guide to
    Spiritual Enlightenment*
    (Tolle), 57
The Power of Now Exercises
    (Tolle), 193
pride, 36–37

privacy issues and saving face,
    15–16, 18
projection and mirroring, 33
protection, 33

Q
*QBQ! The Question Behind
    the Question: Practicing
    Personal Accountability in
    Work and in Life* (Miller),
    154
Quiet Your Mind (Selby), 57
quizzes
    accountability, 152–53
    apologies, 101–2
    being judgmental, 40–42
    communication style, 170–72
    coping skills, 191–92
    differences and similarities
        between nuclear mom,
        stepmom, or ex-wife, 21–23
    difficult emotions, 24–26,
        221–22
    fears about getting along,
        78–80
    finger-pointing, 146–47
    ongoing problems between
        mom/stepmom, 135–37
    present feelings of hope, 81
    supporting the kids' interests
        and hobbies, 199–201
    willingness to make changes,
        113–14

R

Radical Collaboration: Five Essential Skills to Overcome Defensiveness and Build Successful Relationships (Tamm and Luyet), 137

rational thinking, 186–87

recognition, value of, 215–16

regrouping, 174–93

The Relationship Cure: A 5-Step Guide to Strengthening Your Marriage, Family and Friendships (Gottman), 225

resentments, 5, 28–29, 46

Rivers, Dennis, 167–68

rules, between houses, 72, 129–34

S

self-absorption, 67–68

self-analysis and self-improvement, 55–56, 184–86

The Seven Challenges Workbook: Cooperative Communication Skills for Success at Home and at Work (Rivers), 167–68

The 7 Habits of Highly Effective Families (Covey), 82

shadow self (hidden self), 31–33, 35–40

The Shelter of Each Other: Rebuilding Our Families (Pipher), 114, 208

simplicity, 109

SouleMama web site, 225

Stepfamily Foundation web site, 27

Stepfamily Letter Project web site, 173

Stepwives: Ten Steps to Help Ex-Wives and Step-Mothers End the Struggle and Put the Kids First (Oxhorn, Oxhorn-Ringwood and Krausz), 26

Steve Pavlina's Personal Development for Smart People web site, 57

strategizing, 7

stress
and breathing, 93, 178–79, 181
and emotions, 6, 11
and exercise, 187–88
managing, 92–93
and meditation, 186
self-generated, 189–90
and sleep, 190

superiority, 37, 51

surveys, worries, 123–24

T

Taming Your Gremlin web site, 193

Ten Zen Seconds (Maisel), 181–83, 193

territoriality, 5, 7, 183

Thank You for Being Such a Pain: Spiritual Guidance for Dealing with Difficult People (Rosen), 57
32 Keys web site, 57
Tolle, Eckhardt, 185–86
traits, shadow side, 35–40
truces, 97–99
trust, 145–46

V
Values Parenting web site, 225
verbal digs, 92
victimhood, 38
visualization, 202–3
vulnerability, 150

W
web sites, resources, 26, 57, 82, 115, 138, 154, 173, 193, 208, 225
what-if fantasies, 49–51
Wild Mind web site, 115

Y
yielding, 89–90

Z
Zen Habits web site, 154, 208

Acknowledgments

We owe our incredible team of reviewers a huge debt of gratitude. They used their eagle eyes and genius brains to strengthen our material—and usually on a weekend, at that! Big thanks to: Joanna Cordry, Kimberly Cockrill, Beckett Gilchrist, Aliza Gold, Kelly Young Gray, Kris Marr, Karen Owens, Gregg Roberts, Sarah Schopp, Carla Feldpausch, Christie Smith, Leanne Stahnke, and Holly VanScoy.

Thanks to our agent Sharlene Martin for believing in our book and coming out of the gate with a bang. To our editor, Heather Carreiro, and the wonderful team at Globe (Himeka Curiel and Robert Sembiante, in particular), thank you for your enthusiasm and encouragement—it's a nice feeling, knowing we're in such capable hands.

Special thanks to the multi-talented Regan Brown, who generously lent us her professional expertise and evaluated an early draft of our proposal, and to neurologist Dr. David Morledge for his earnest attempts to keep Jennifer's brain working and migraine-free.

Thanks to writer and MediaBistro instructor Wendy Goldman Rohm for incisive guidance, and to the students of our nonfiction class for cheerleading and reviews.

We couldn't have done it without supportive, treasured friends, such as the Austin Writergrrls, Climbing Buddies, Jonathan Singer, Michele Hallahan, Nathan Havlick, Barry Landry and Dan Ruiz, Kim Lane, Don Piper and Laura Poe, Kai Woodfin, and Penny Van Horn. Friends who pulled double-duty as both emergency therapists *and* reviewers included: Brenton Buxton, Liesbet Collaert, Pippa Gaubert, Jane Gramzinski, Rebecca Lincoln, Chris Pye, Patricia Talbert, and Karl Vochatzer. Thanks y'all, from the heart.

Our love and thanks go to our respective families, who matched us in excitement as this project came to fruition.

To David, husband to Carol and father of Jennifer's children, thank you for trusting us with all your secrets! And thank you for trusting us enough to develop a true friendship while bringing our families closer together.

And finally, to the kids, thank you for putting up with us while we were distracted and sometimes grumpy and unavailable. You are our joy and inspiration—and the whole reason for this book! We love you.

About the Authors

Jennifer Newcomb Marine is a freelance writer and editor. Her credits include *Grrl Talk: Wit, Sass and Wisdom from the Austin Writergrrls*. She has presented workshops on parenting and creativity, and taught video production classes to children and teens (including first-time offenders). She's an avid traveler (especially with her two teenage daughters), rock climber, and rower. Catch up with her various projects at www.jennifernewcombmarine.com.

Carol Marine is a successful fine artist whose work has been featured in national publications, as well as a variety of galleries. Her "A Painting a Day" site (www.carolmarine.blogspot.com) has an avid following and her international painting workshops often sell out months in advance. She's a passionate photographer and outdoor enthusiast who manages to stay in shape by running, hiking, and chasing around a very active three year-old son.

For more information on strengthening your mother/stepmother relationship, check us out at www.noonesthebitch.com.